Artimals

Coloring the Whimsical Wild

Written & Illustrated by: Kara Mae Adamo

Adamo Publishing
& Artsy Pixie Media, LLC

Artimals; Coloring the Whimsical Wild

Published by Adamo Publishing; Artsy Pixie Media, LLC
1607 East Ridgewood Street| Orlando, Florida| 32803

Edited by *N. P. Thompson*

Published in the United States of America

ISBN: 978-0-692-58855-0

Environment, Animal Conservation & Art

Arts&Crafts/Education

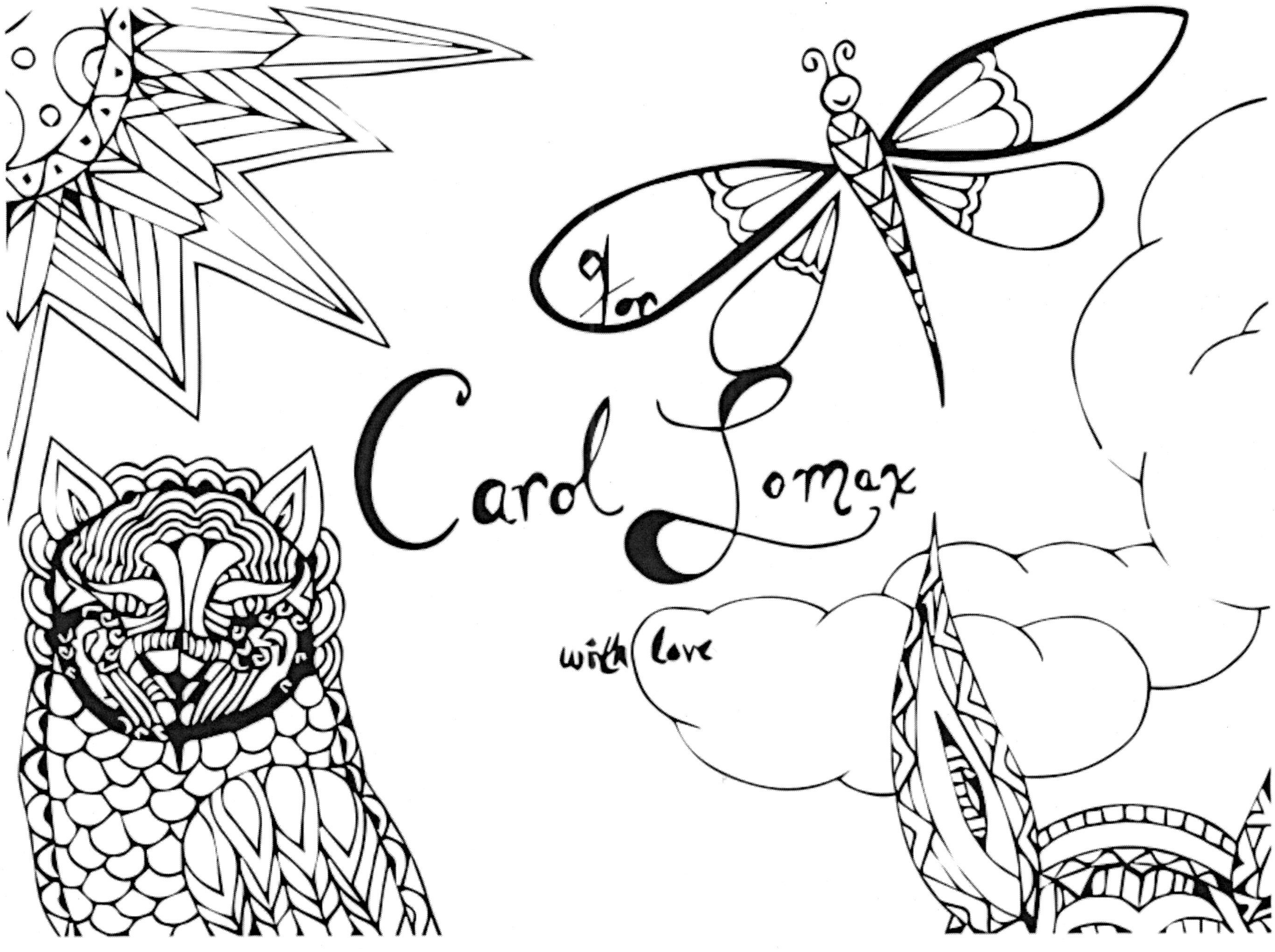
For
Carol Lomax
with love

Table of Contents

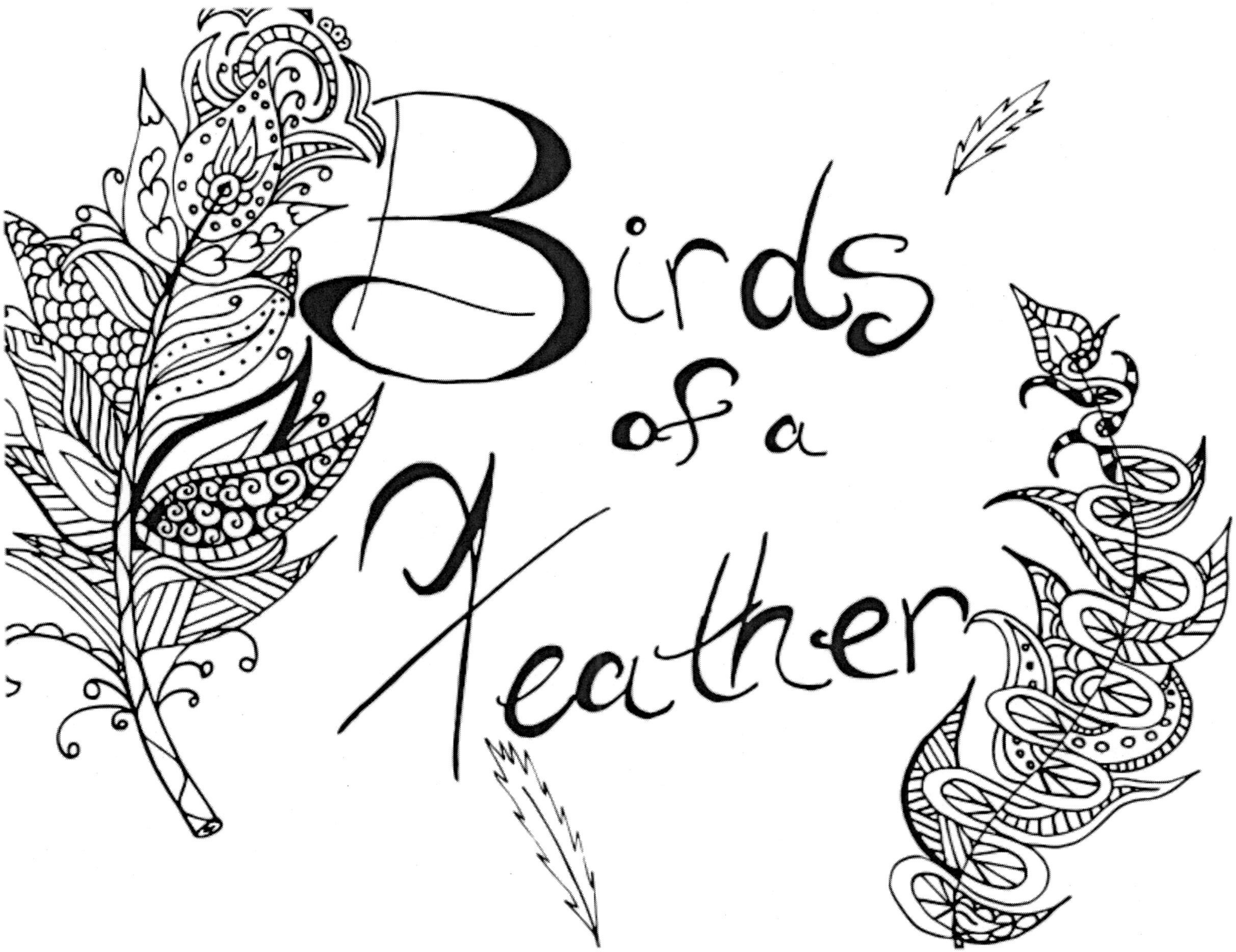
Birds of a Feather

Mallard

- **Fun Facts**
  - The average lifespan of a mallard duck is 20 years.
  - They can grow up to 3-1/2 lbs.
  - Male mallard ducks are referred to as *drakes.*
  - Drakes are more distinctly colored than female mallards.
  - Females normally lay about a dozen eggs.
  - Mallards take about a month to hatch.
  - Mallards are thought to be the most abundant duck on Earth.
  - The mallard is the ancestor of most domestic duck breeds.
- **What Do They Eat?**
  - Mallards usually eat fish, amphibians, and a variety of plants and grains found in the water and on land.
- **Where They Hang Out**
  - Mallards are attracted to calm bodies of water. They can be found throughout Asia, Europe, and North America. Generally, they like to stay in the subtropics.
- **Helpful Organization**
  - Ducks Unlimited

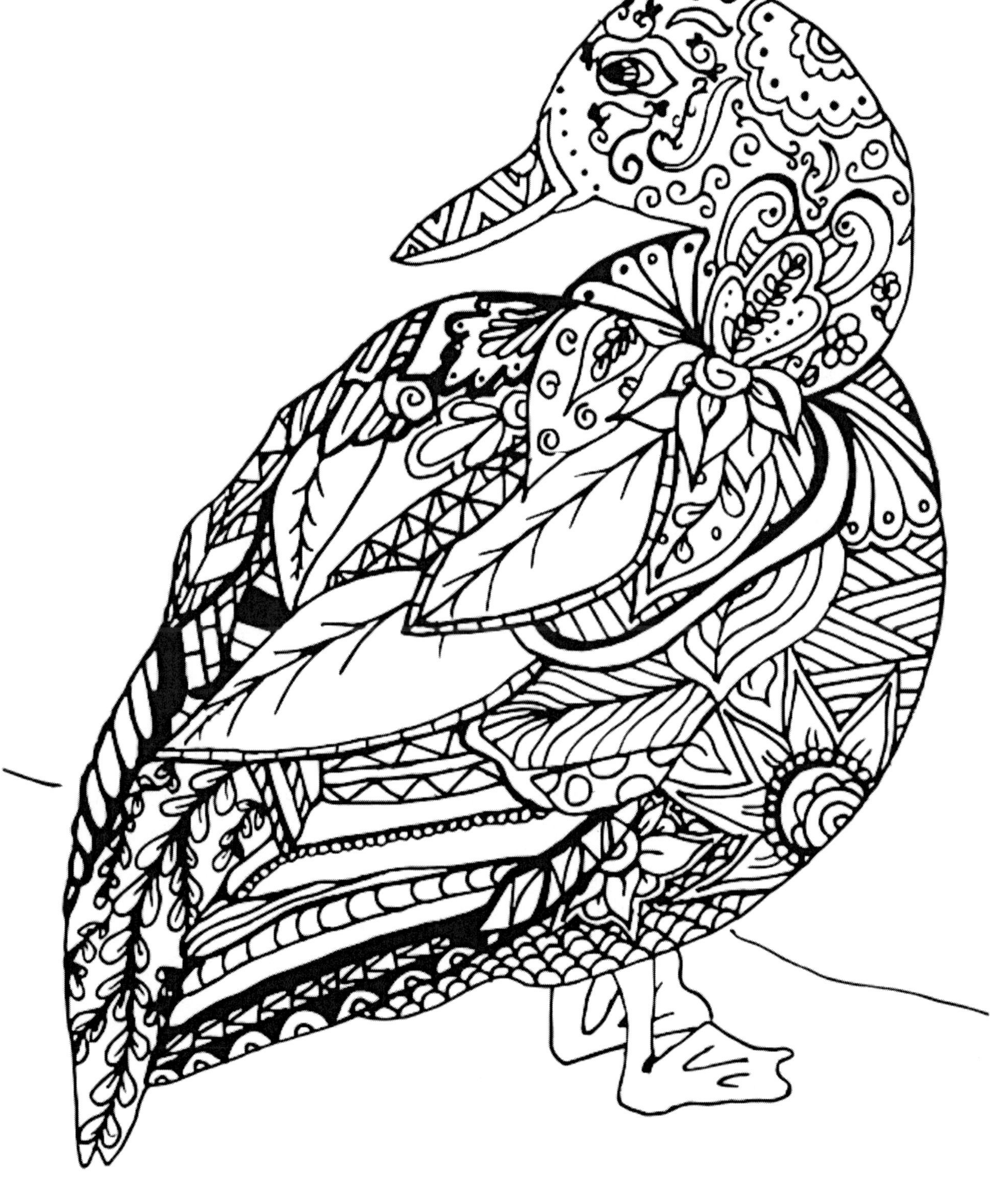

Parrot

- **Fun Facts**
  - The average lifespan of a parrot is around 80 years and they can grow up to about 4 lbs.
  - Many species of parrots are monogamous and work together to raise their young.
  - Parrots are usually very social creatures. In the wild they've been known to hang out in groups of 20 or more.
  - Parrots usually lay between 2 and 8 eggs at a time & the take about a month to hatch.
  - Parrots are excellent mimics. They can learn human words and can copy laughter.
  - Many parrots are endangered.
- **What Do They Eat?**
  - Parrots usually eat nuts, seeds, flowers, fruit, insects, and buds.
- **Where They Hang Out**
  - Parrots generally like warmer climates like Mexico, Australia, South America, and Central America. There are also a few cold-weather varieties that prefer the snow.
- **Helpful Organizations**
  - Kakapo Recovery Organization
  - World Parrot Trust
  - Parrot Preservation Society

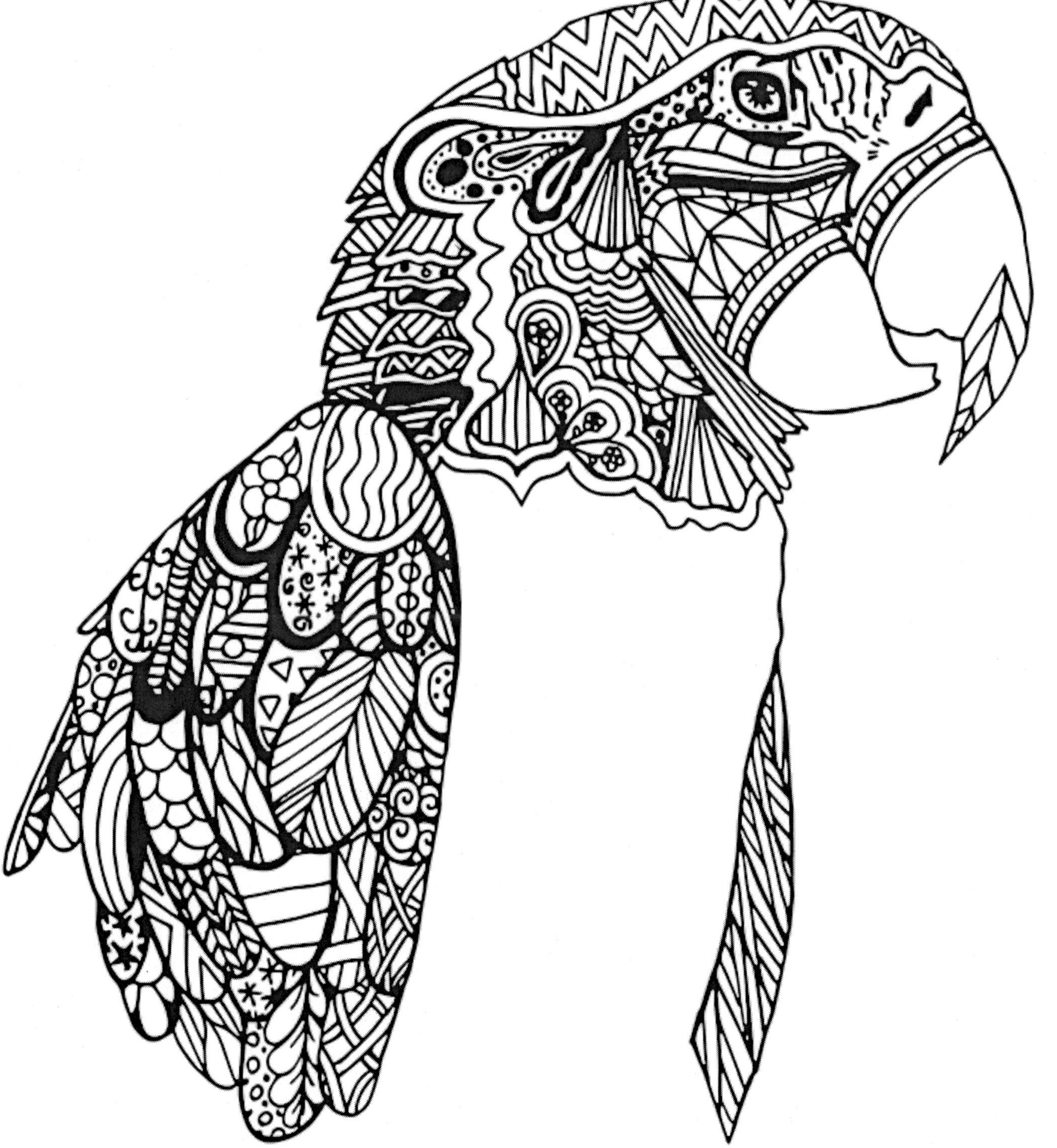

Swan

- **Fun Facts**
  - Swans can fly up to 60mph.
  - A male swan is called a *cob*, and a female swan is called a *pen*.
  - They can grow up to 24-26 lbs.
  - Swans usually lay between 3 and 9 eggs at a time and they take about a month to hatch.
  - Swans aren't generally monogamous, but they usually keep a special bond with their mates and often stay together for a few years.
  - Swans are considered threatened. This is mainly because of pollution, habitat loss, and hunting.
  - Swans are highly intelligent and will remember if individuals are nice to them or not.
- **What do they Eat?**
  - Swans eat aquatic plants, insects, and small fish.
- **Where They Hang Out**
  - Swans like large, shallow wetlands and open water.
- **Helpful Organizations**
  - Northwest Swan Association
  - The Trumpeter Swan Society

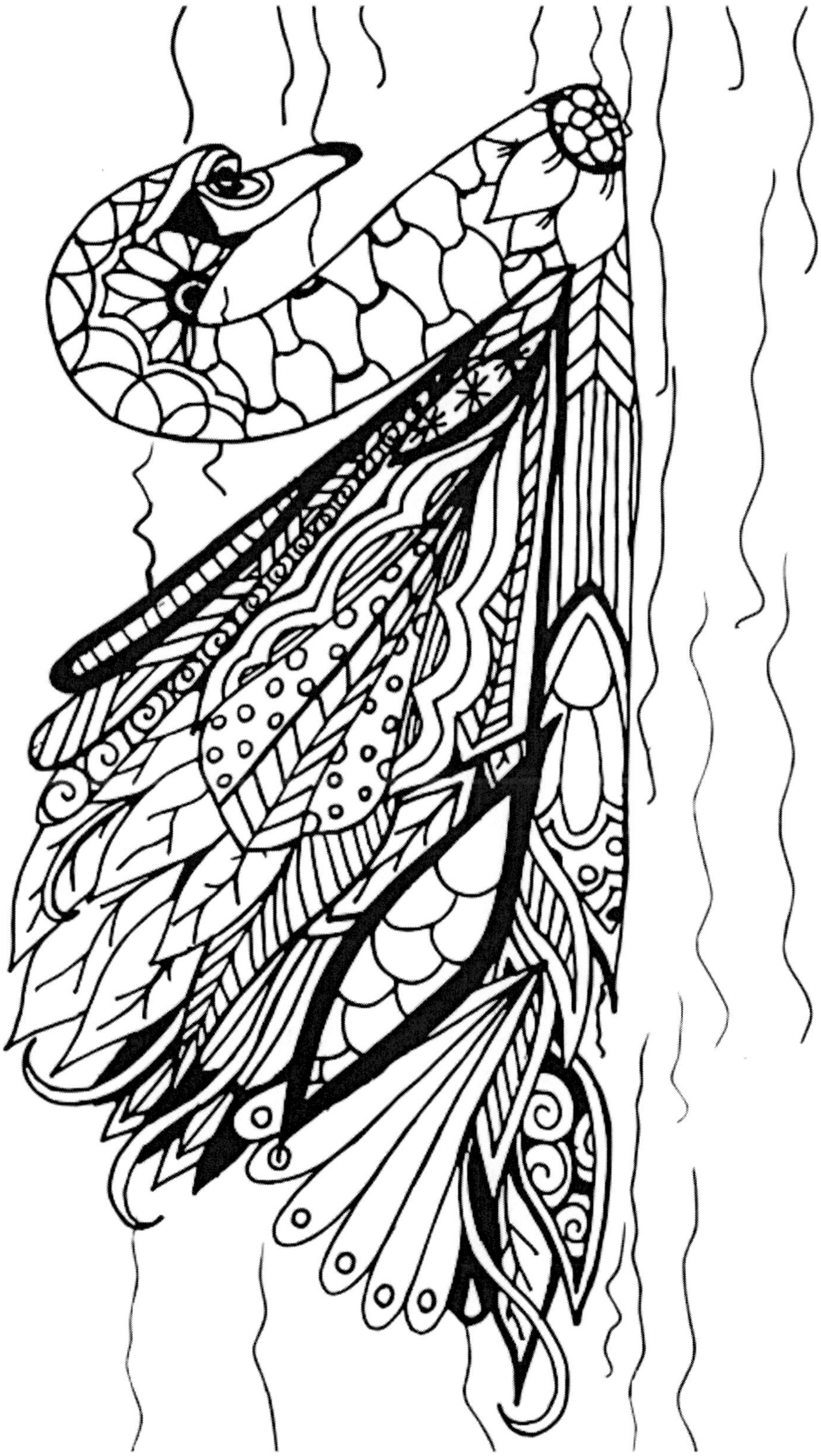

Chickens

- **Fun Facts**
  - Chickens can distinguish between more than 100 faces of their own species and even remember each other.
  - Chickens form "pecking orders" in social circles and every one of them knows and acknowledges their place on the social ladder.
  - Chickens see in full color.
  - Chickens experience REM sleep like we do—that means they dream when they are sleeping!
  - Chickens have pain receptors similar to ours—so they feel pain and distress like humans.
  - Chickens are fiercely protective over their young. They even talk to them while they are still in their eggs, teaching their children calls before they even hatch.
- **What Do They Eat?**
  - Chickens eat vegetables, fruits, flowers, grass, and bugs.
- **Where They Hang Out**
  - Chickens originally came from India and South-East Asia. Now they are all over Europe and North America
- **Helpful Organizations**
  - The Livestock Conservancy
  - Western Association of Fish & Wildlife Agencies (WAFWA)

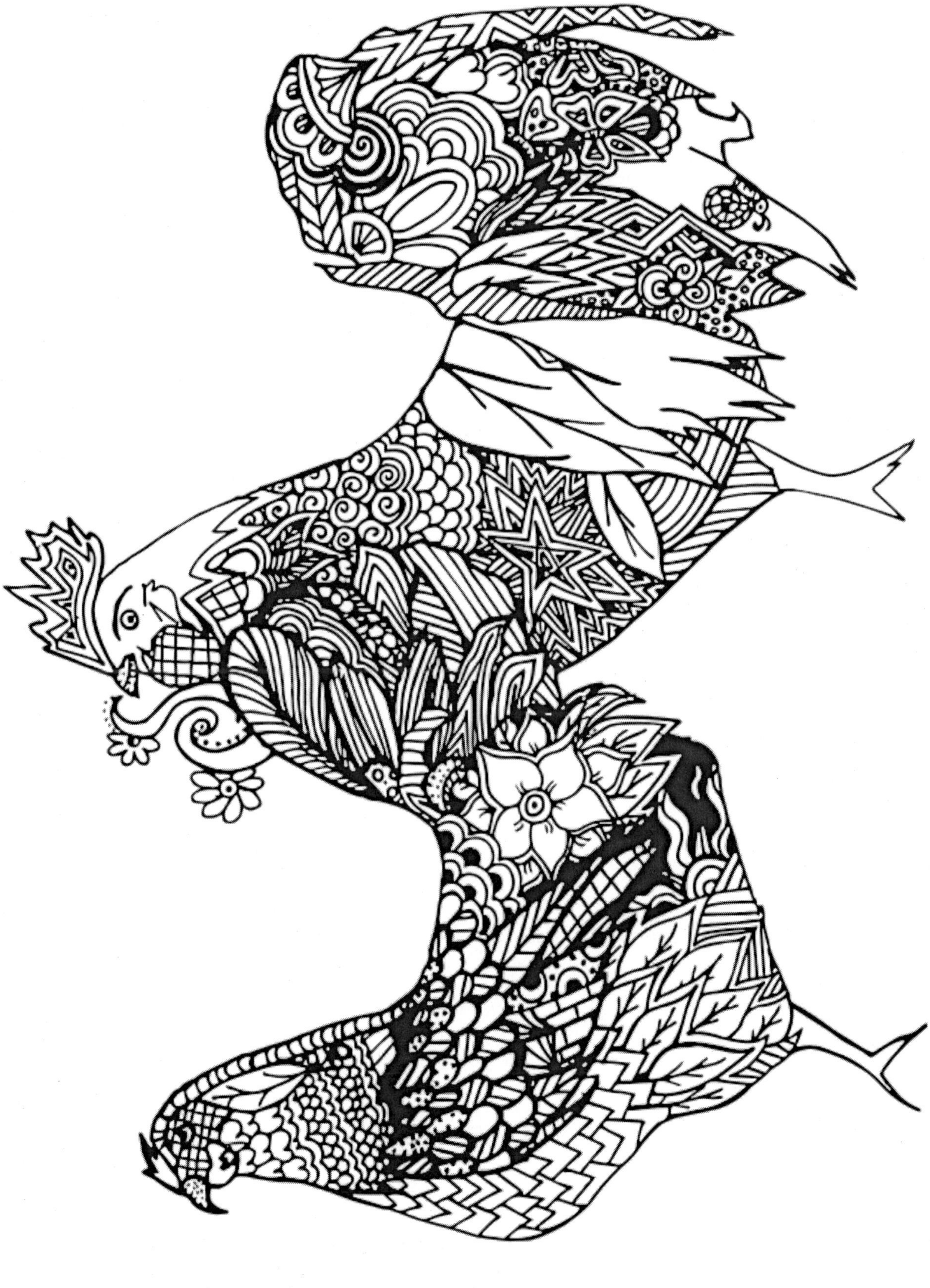

Owl

- **Fun Facts**
  - There are about 205 species of owls. These are divided into two groups: Barn Owls and the True Owls.
  - Barn Owls have a heart-shaped face and long legs. There are 16 species of Barn Owls.
  - True Owls have round faces, short tails and large heads.
  - Owls are generally solitary, nocturnal birds.
  - In Kenya, the Kikuyu tribe once believed that owls were harbingers of death. They are often viewed as signs of bad luck or ill health—a superstition that carries over into literature and films.
  - In Seminole and Apache tribes, children are told that, if they cry too much at night, owls will carry them away. In other North American Tribes, owls are associated with the *spirits of the dead,* and the bony circles around their eyes are supposed to be made up of fingernails of apparitional humans. Spooky.
- **What Do They Eat?**
  - Owls hunt insects, other birds, and small mammals. Some species also eat fish.
- **Where They Hang Out**
  - Owls live all over the world. They can be found on every continent except Antarctica.
- **Helpful Organization**
  - The World Owl Trust (WOT)

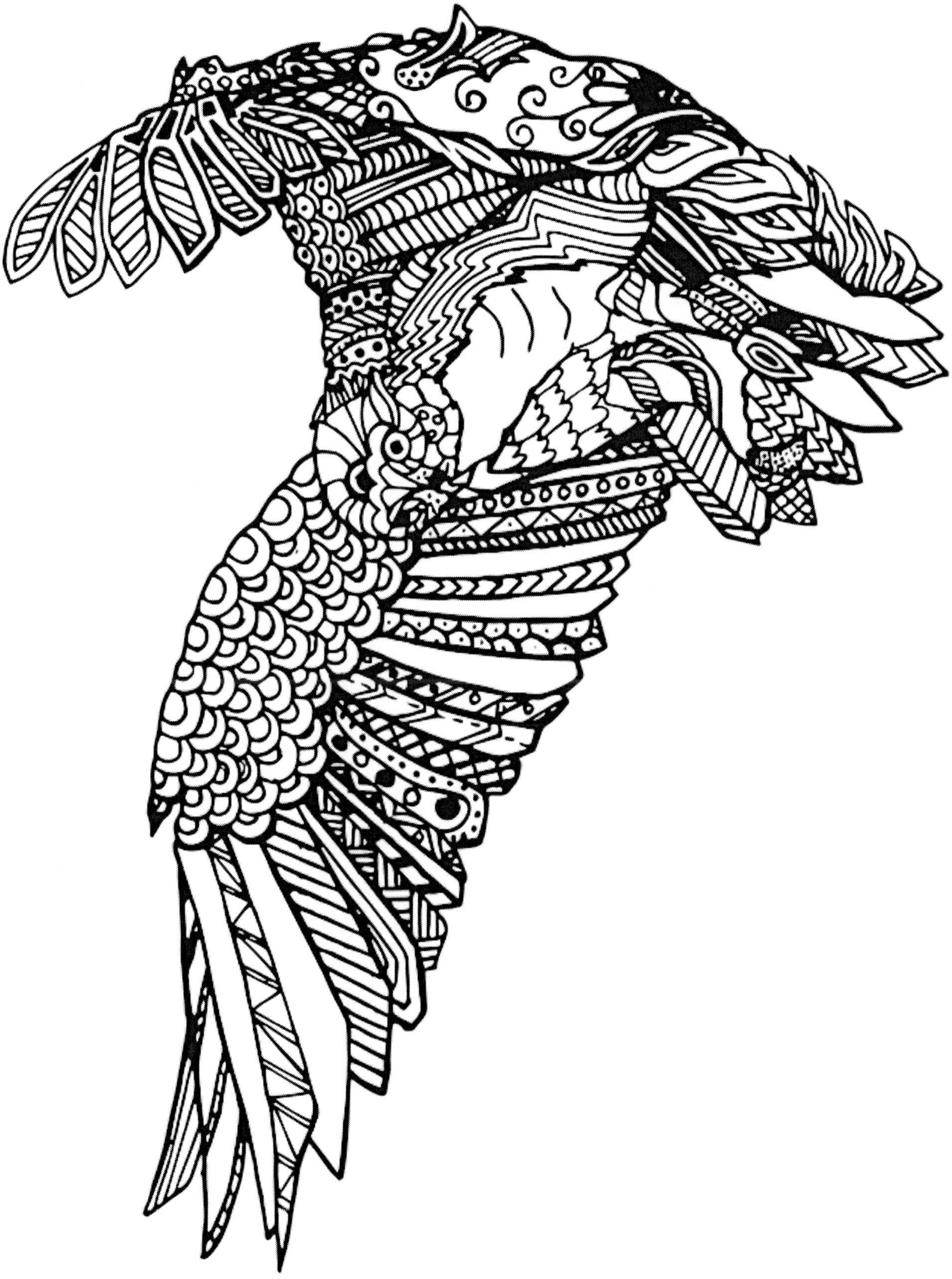

Peacock

- **Fun Facts**
  - Peacocks live an average of 20 years.
  - Male peacocks mate with several females in their lifetime and the females usually lay 3 to 5 eggs at a time.
  - Peacocks don't really get along well with other birds.
  - Only the males are actually called *peacocks.* The birds, altogether, are referred to as *peafowl.* Females are *peahens,* and the babies are called *peachicks.*
  - A family of peafowl is called a *brevy.*
  - Peacocks shed their train after mating season, so the feathers can be gathered & sold without hurting the birds.
  - Peacocks can fake their copulatory call, making it look like they are mating more than they actually are. They do this to trick females into thinking they're more desirable than their rivals. They seriously fake it.
- **What do they Eat?**
  - Peacocks eat insects and plants.
- **Where They Hang Out**
  - The blue-feathered peacock lives in India and Sri Lanka, while the green peacock is found in Java and Burma.
- **Helpful Organization**
  - World Wildlife Fund

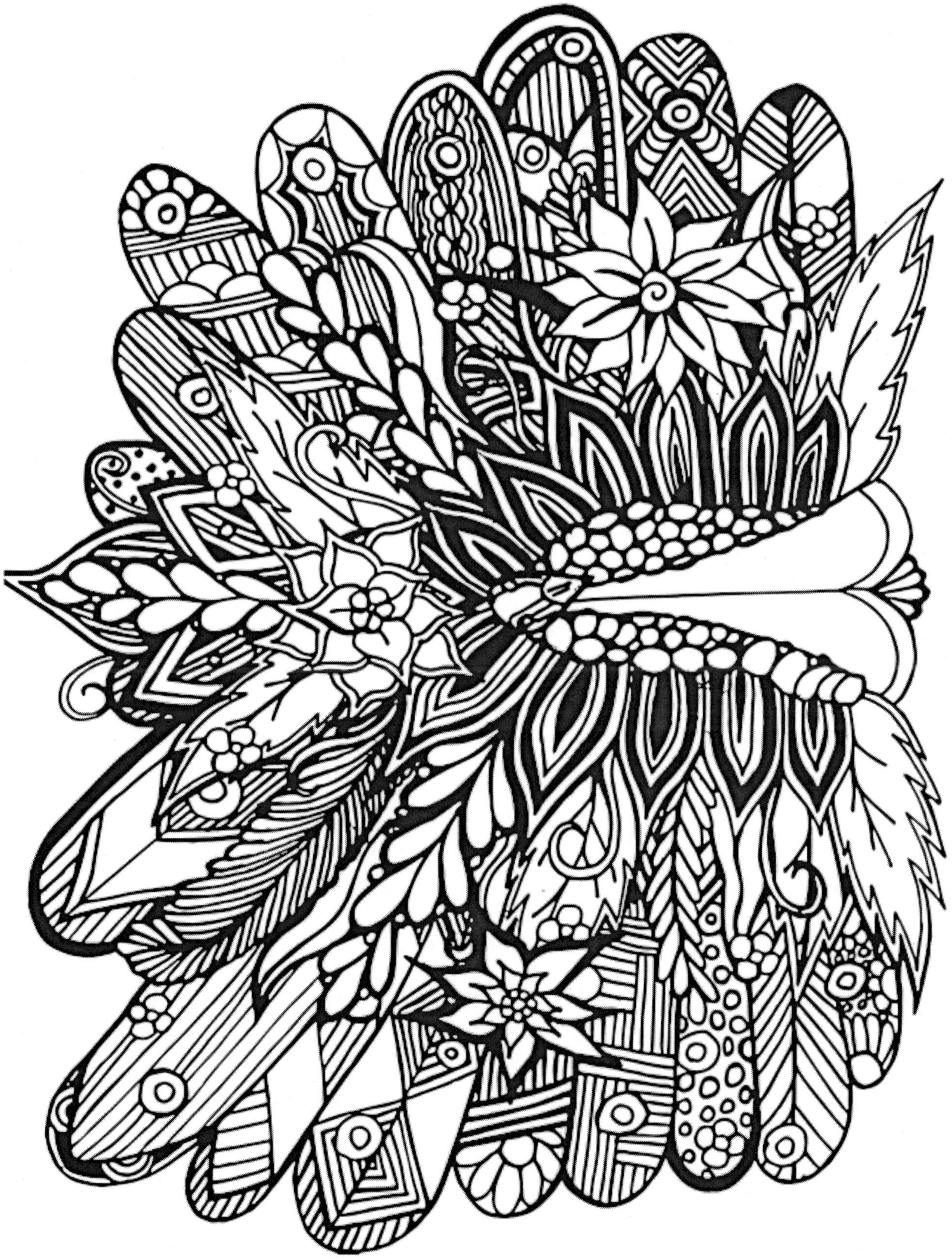

Hawk

- **Fun Facts**
  - Hawks have sharp, curved talons and strong beaks that are hooked for biting and tearing flesh.
  - Hawks can fly up to 150 mph when diving after their prey.
  - Their eyesight is considered the best of any known animal on earth; they can see 8 times clearer than we do!
  - Female hawks are larger than male hawks. Large hawks lay from 1-2 eggs per year. Small hawks lay 3-5.
  - It is illegal to capture, kill, or possess a hawk, (dead or alive), without proper permits.
  - Small hawks grow to full size within a month. Larger species take about 11 weeks.
  - There are approximately 17 species of hawks in North America alone.
- **What Do They Eat?**
  - Hawks are carnivorous. They eat rodents, small animals, snakes, small birds, and various fish.
- **Where They Hang Out**
  - Hawks are forest raptors. They live near swamps and up in conifer forests. They like open sub-canopies so they can hunt easily. They can be found throughout North & Central America and in the West Indies.
- **Helpful Organizations**
  - The Raptor Trust
  - Hawks Aloft, Inc.

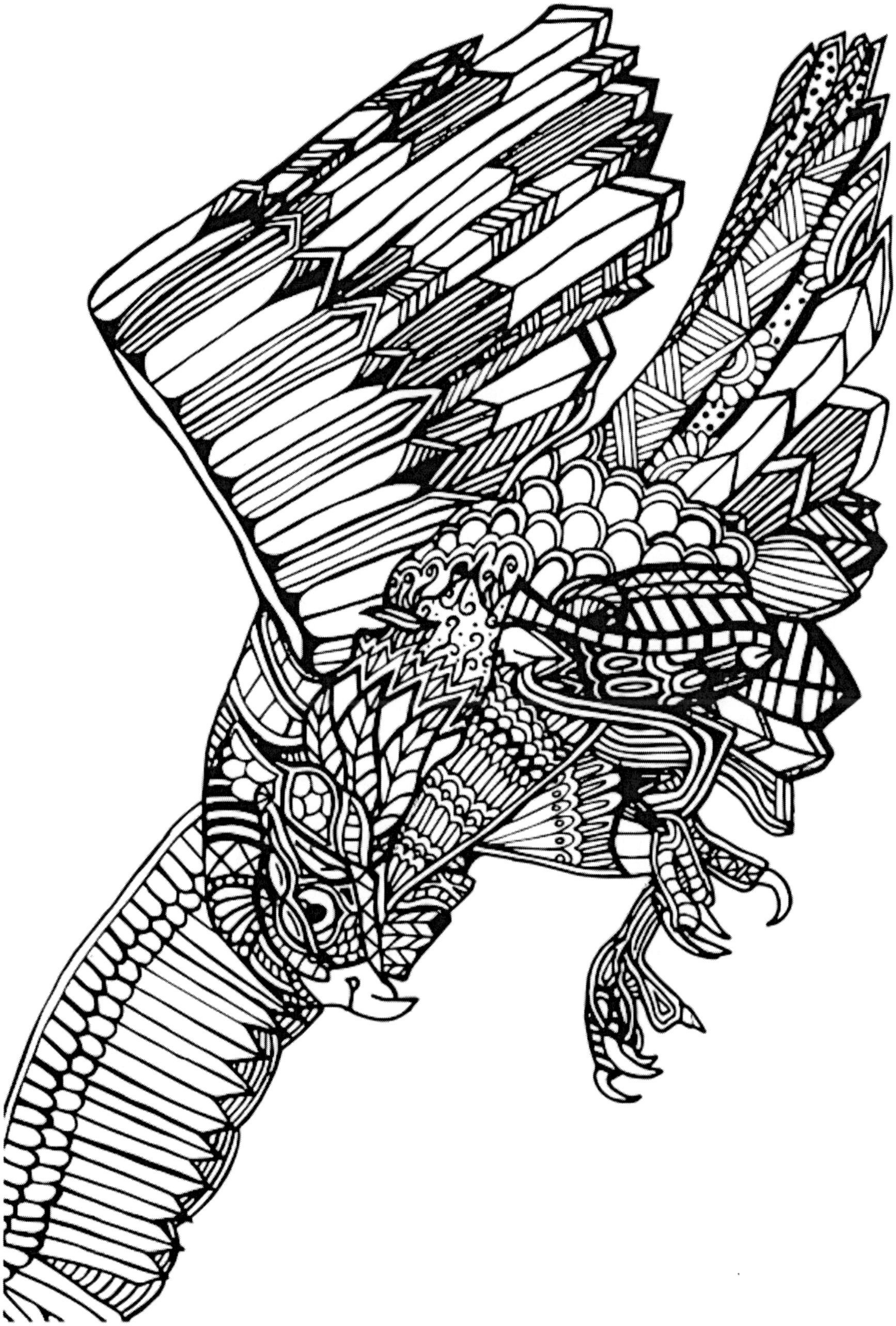

Penguins

- **Fun Facts**
  - Penguins are aquatic birds that spend up to75% of their time in the water.
  - The "tuxedo shading" on penguins is referred to as *counter-shading*, which is a form of camouflage that helps keep them safe when they're in the water.
  - Penguins have a distinct call that allows them to locate their mate and their young in large groups of up to thousands of other penguins.
  - They raise their young on land.
  - Penguins are social birds: they nest, swim, and feed in groups.
  - King and Emperor Penguins lay one egg. All of the other penguins lay two.
  - Penguins live between 15-20 years, depending on the species.
- **What Do They Eat?**
  - Penguins eat krill, squid, and fish.
- **Where They Hang Out**
  - Penguins are mainly found throughout the Southern Hemisphere
- **Helpful Organization**
  - International Penguin Conservation Work Group

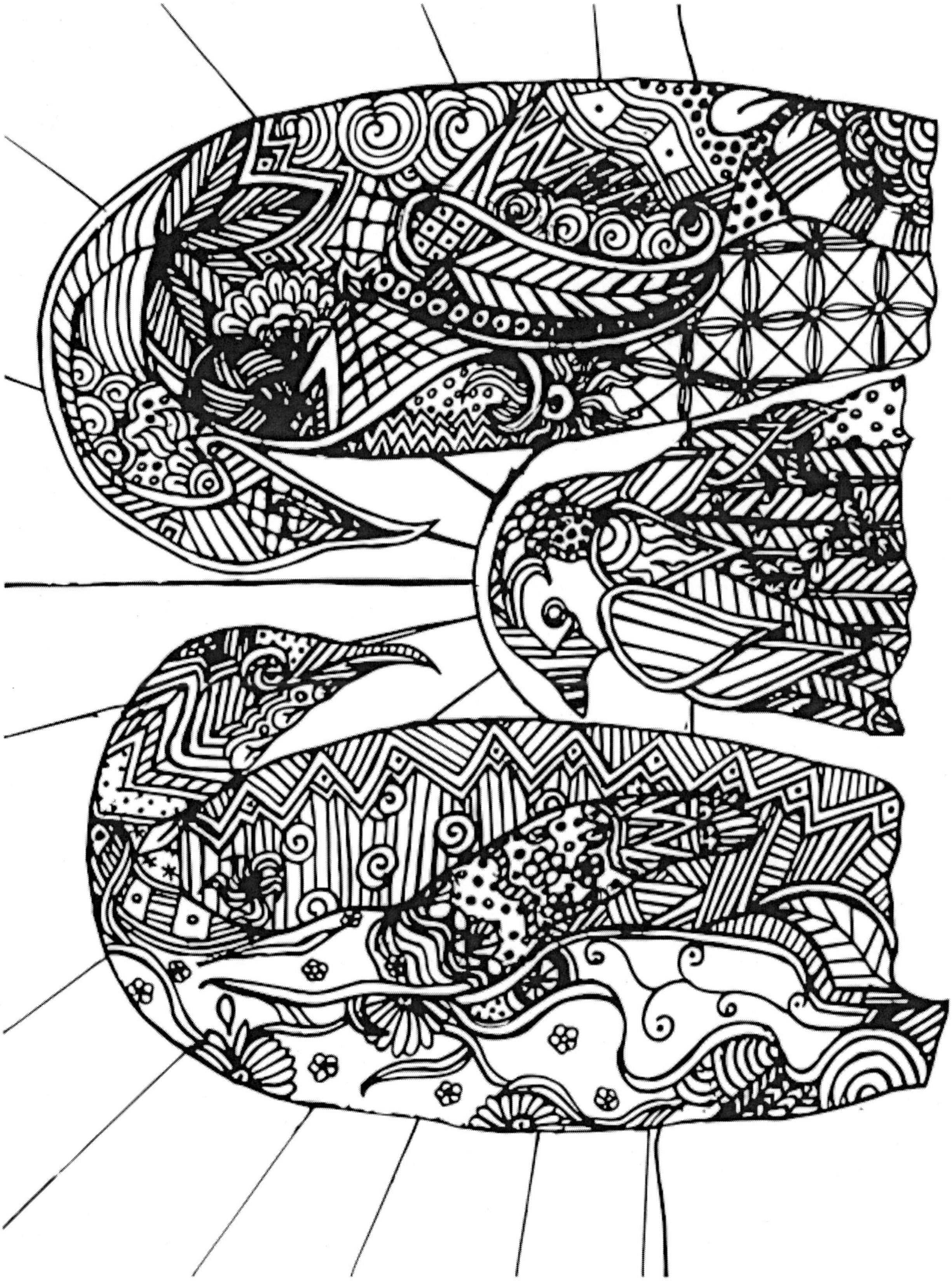

Eagle

- **Fun Fact**
  - The *Bald Eagle* is the official bird of the United States of America and is fiercely protected. Killing an eagle is an immediate felony.
  - There are more than 60 different species of eagle
  - Eagles generally lay two eggs, but the older and larger chick will kill off its younger sibling. The parents do not intervene when this happens.
  - Native Americans historically presented eagle feathers non-indigenous people and members of other tribes. The gift was symbolic of acceptance and respect and was only given to those deemed worthy of the honor.
  - The Aztecs would build cities only where an eagle would land.
- **What Do They Eat?**
  - The African Vulturine Fish-Eagle is a vegetarian that eats rich palm fruits. The rest are carnivorous.
- **Where They Hang Out**
  - Eagles can be found on every continent on Earth. They generally nest high up in mature trees.
- **Helpful Organizations**
  - National Eagle Center
  - Eagle Nature Foundation

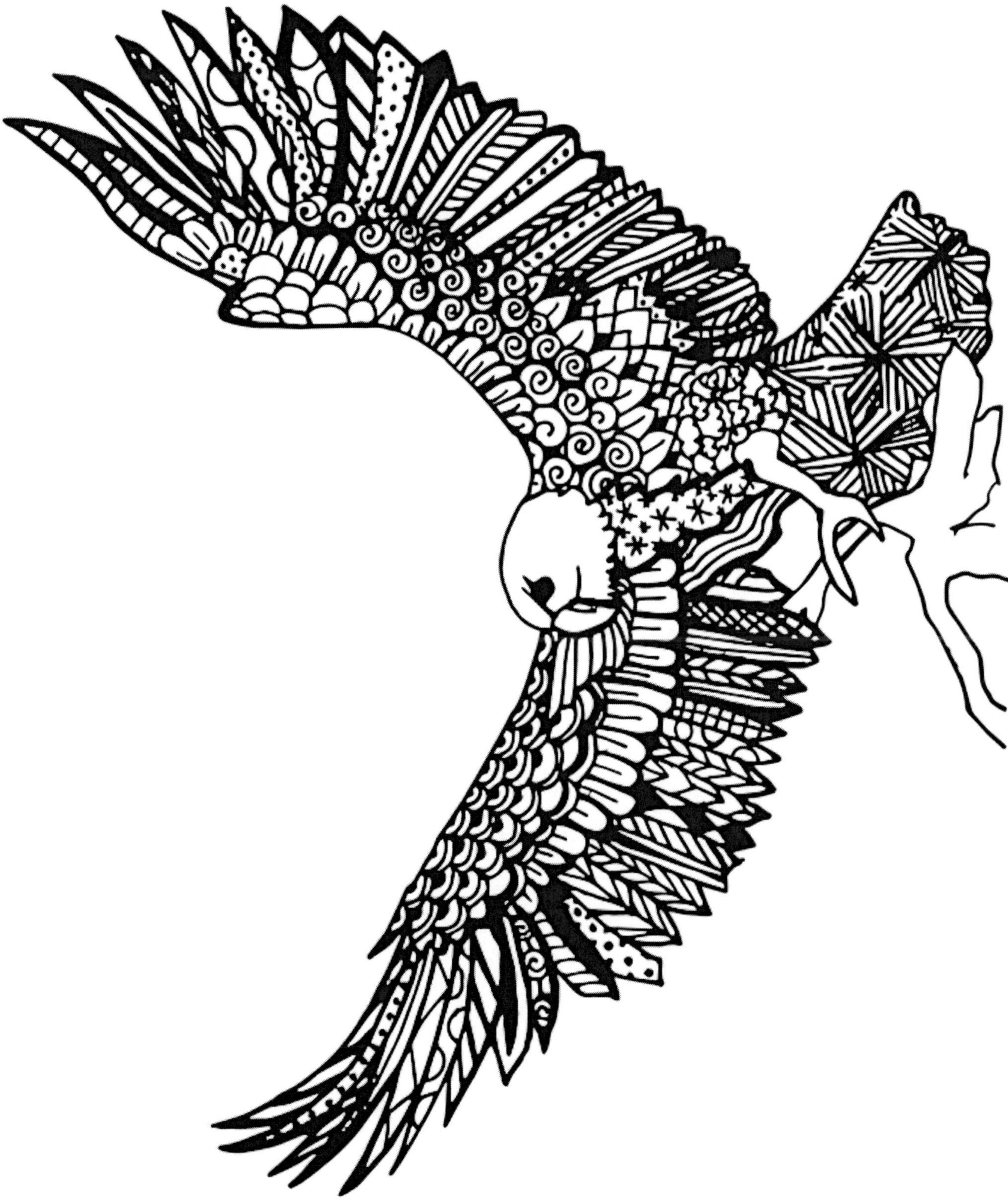

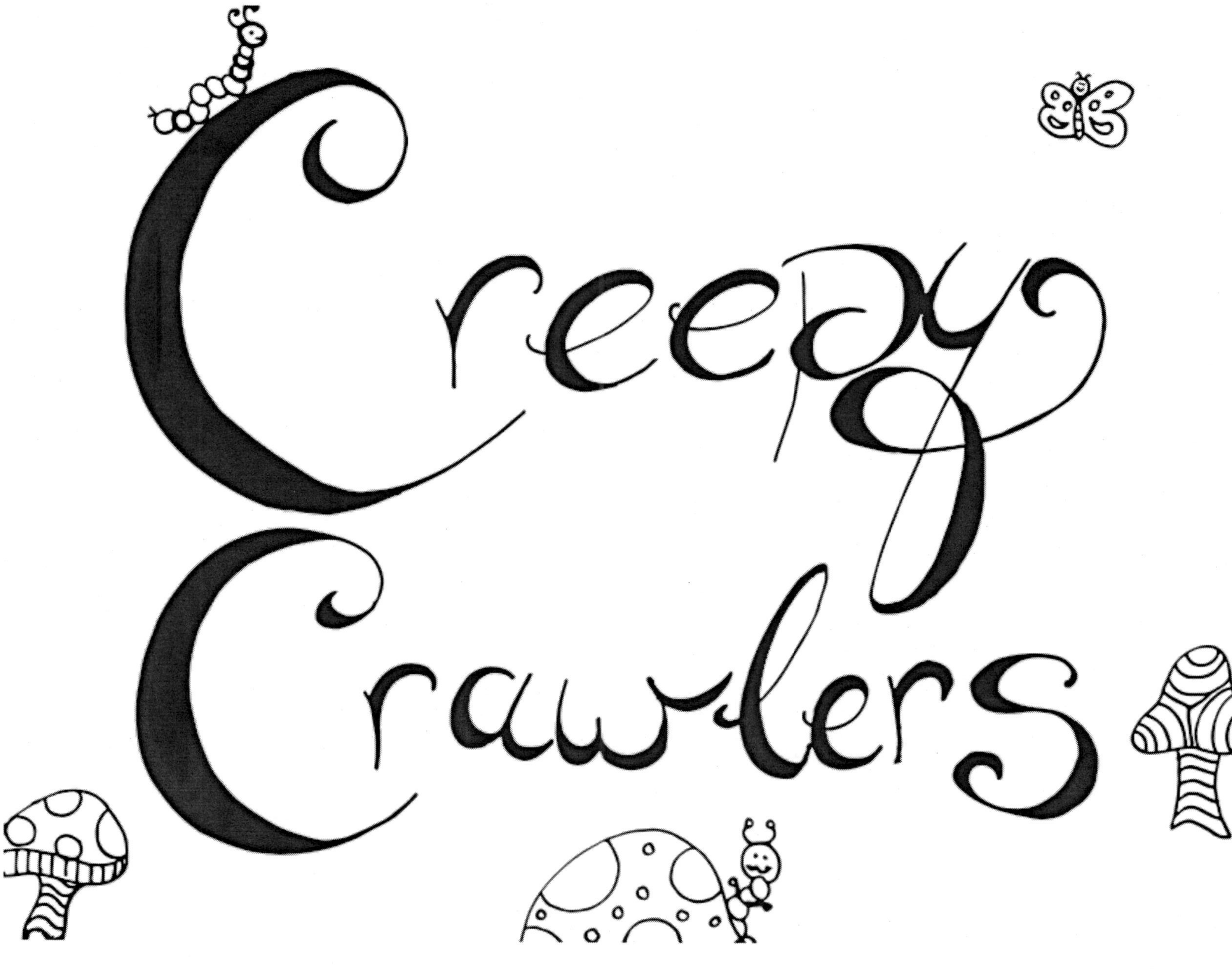
Creepy
Crawlers

Butterfly

- **Fun Facts**
  - Studies have shown that butterflies, which basically turn to mush while transforming in their cocoons, still somehow retain memories during that transformation.
  - Some butterflies are only an 1/8" from wing-to-wing, while others can grow up to almost 12"
  - Butterflies can fly up to 12 miles per hour. They can only fly if their body temperature is above 86 degrees.
  - There are about 24,000 species of butterflies.
  - Every year, to escape the bitter cold, Monarch Butterflies travel from the Great Lakes to the Gulf of Mexico, (about 2,000 miles), and return to the north in the spring.
  - Some people say that, when the black bands on a Woolybear Caterpillar are wide, a cold winter is coming.
- **What Do They Eat?**
  - When Butterflies are still caterpillars, they only eat leaves of plants. Once they are butterflies, they consume nectar, water, and liquid from fruits.
- **Where They Hang Out**
  - Butterflies can be found on every continent on Earth.
- **Helpful Organization**
  - The Xerces Society

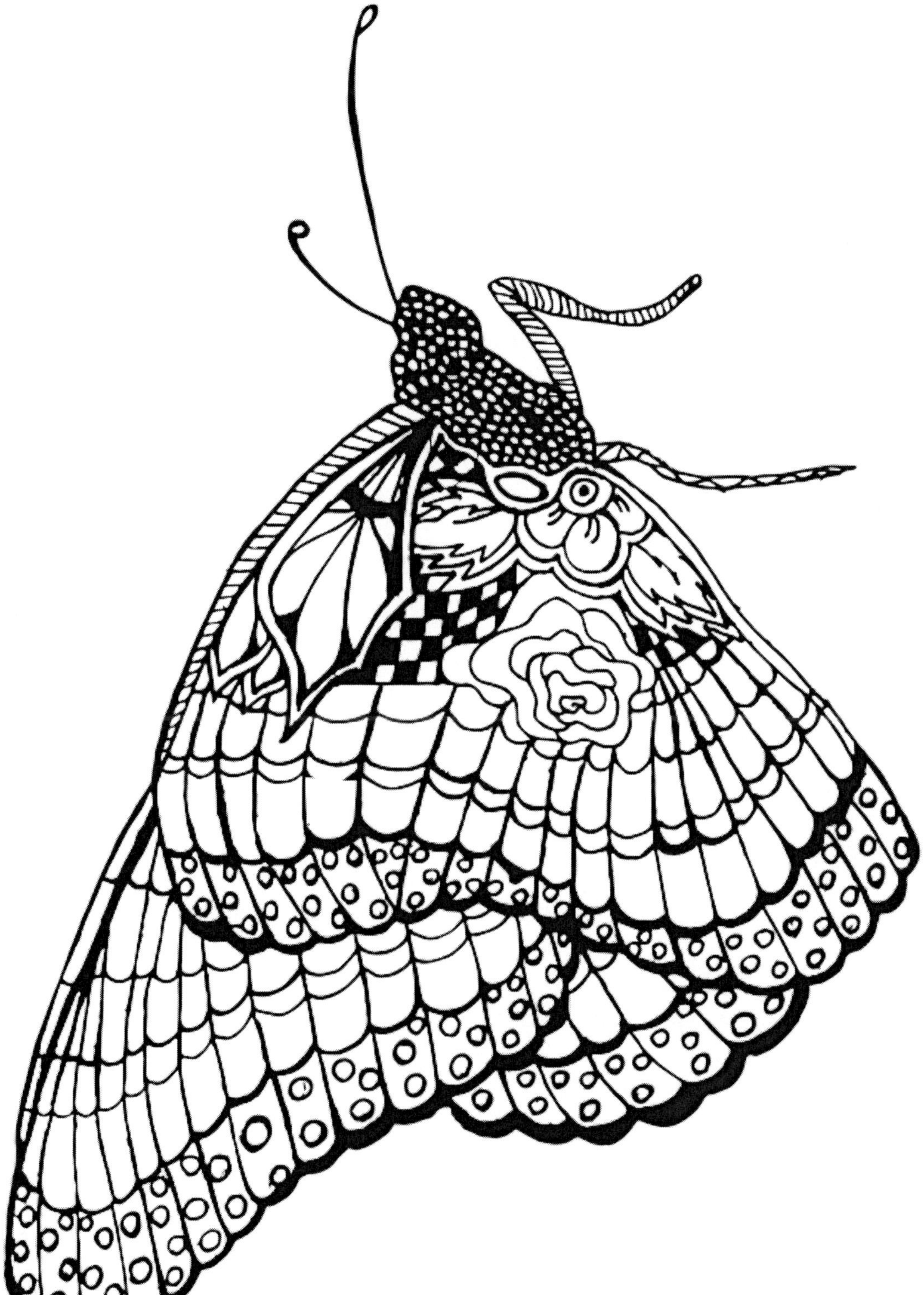

Bumble Bee

- **Fun Facts**
    - There are 3 kinds of bees in a hive: Queen, Worker, and Drone
    - Worker Bees are always female. Drone Bees area always male.
    - If a worker bee uses her stinger, she will die.
    - Bees have two sets of wings. Each wing has tiny teeth that can lock together when the bee is flying.
    - The average life of a honeybee during the working season is between 3 and 6 weeks.
    - Bees communicate through pheromones and through special bee dances.
    - A steep decline in bee populations is concerning because of the direct influence bees have on our food supply. Increased efforts toward conservation have gained much attention in recent years.
- **What Do They Eat?**
    - Bees eat nectar and pollen from flowers.
- **Where They Hang Out**
    - Bees live in complex hives made from beeswax. The hives are often found in hollows of trees near wildflowers.
- **Helpful Organizations**
    - Bumble bee Conservation Trust
    - Honey Bee Program

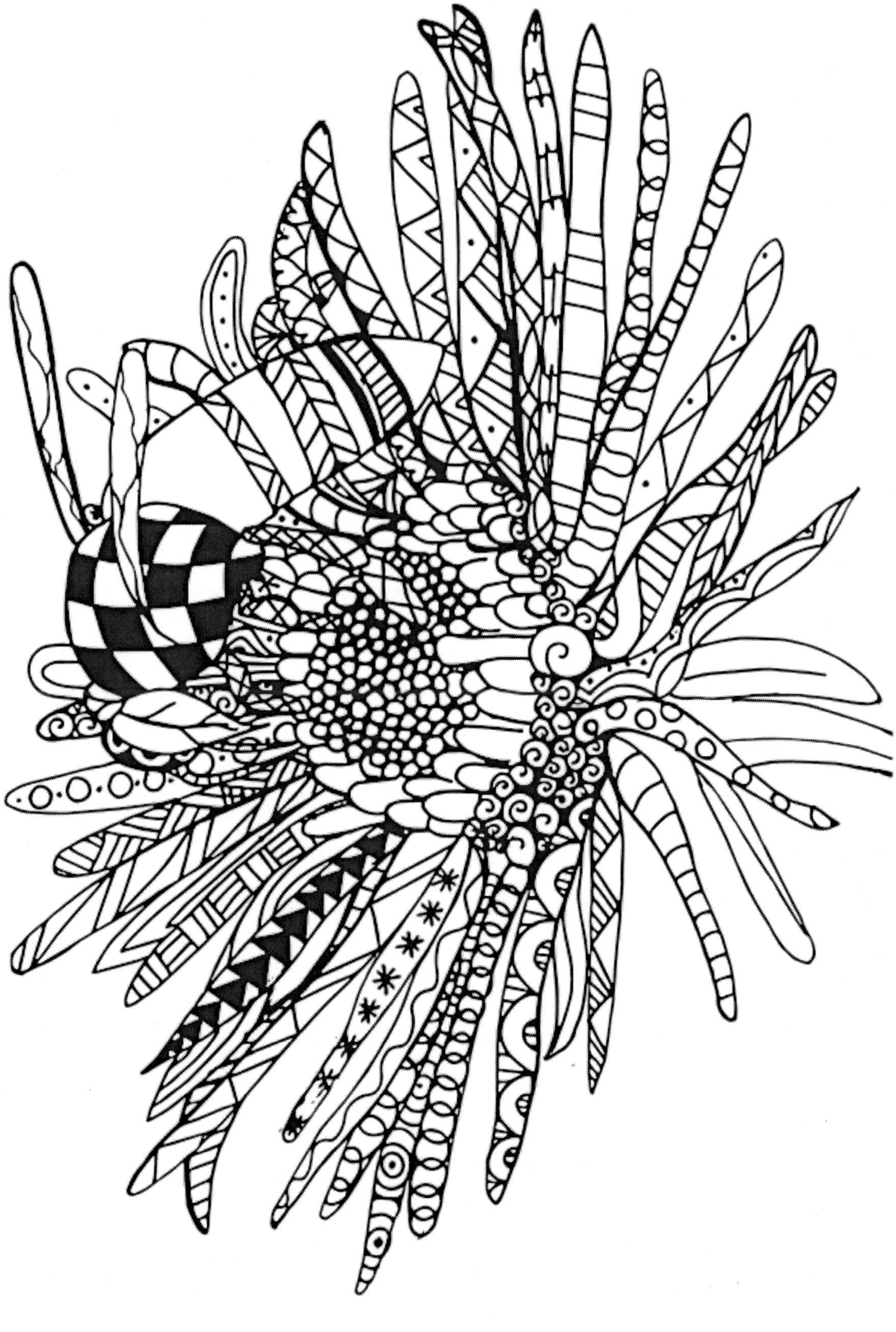

Dragonfly

- **Fun Facts**
  - Dragonflies can fly straight up and down, hover, and even mate mid-air. Their flight patterns are so intricate and impressive that engineers have aspired for years to create robots capable of such patterns.
  - Dragonflies have an enormous eye on top of their head that sees from almost every angle.
  - Fossils of ancient dragonflies from up to 300 million years ago show that they had wingspans of up to 2 feet.
  - Native Americans historically presented eagle feathers non-indigenous people and members of other tribes. The gift was symbolic of acceptance and respect and was only given to those deemed worthy of the honor.
  - There are more than 5,000 known species of dragonflies, all of which have serrated teeth.
- **What Do They Eat?**
  - When they are larvae, they will eat tadpoles, mosquitoes, fish, and other insect larvae. As adults, dragonflies eat other insects. Dragonflies are efficient hunters: they capture between 90-95% of their prey.
- **Where They Hang Out**
  - Dragonflies live around freshwater like lakes and streams. Some of them do travel though. One species actually migrates up to 11,000 miles, which is the longest recorded migration of any other insect on Earth.
- **Helpful Organization**
  - Dragonfly Conservation Group

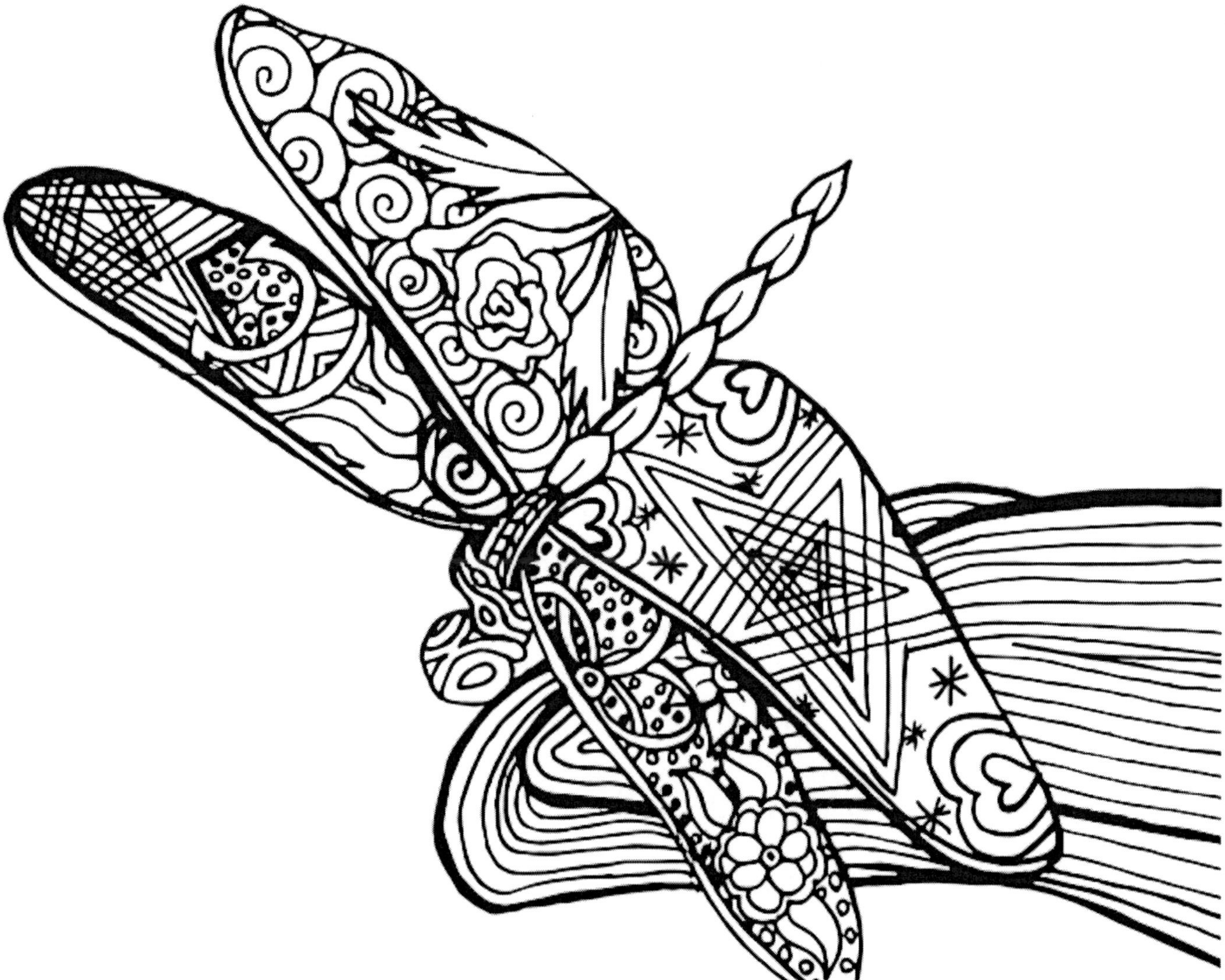

Ladybugs

- **Fun Facts**
  - When threatened, a ladybug will play dead and secrete an unappetizing substance, discouraging predators.
  - Ladybugs smell with their feet and antennae.
  - The color of a ladybugs' spots fade as it gets older.
  - A ladybug's jaws chew side to side instead of up and down.
  - If a ladybug flies, its wings beat up to 85 times per second.
  - When they are larvae, ladybugs resemble tiny alligators with long bodies and bumpy skin.
  - The word "lady" in "ladybug" is in reference to the Virgin Mary. In the middle ages, crops were plagued by pests and the farmers prayed to the Virgin Mary for help. Soon, they started seeing ladybugs in their fields and, at the same time, the crops were somehow saved from the pests. Ladybugs are now thought to bring good fortune.
- **What Do They Eat?**
  - Ladybugs feed on soft-bodied insects like white flies, mites, & aphids. They are also sometimes cannibalistic.
- **Where They Hang Out**
  - Ladybugs live in fields, forests, grasslands and gardens throughout the world.
- **Helpful Organization**
  - The Xerces Society

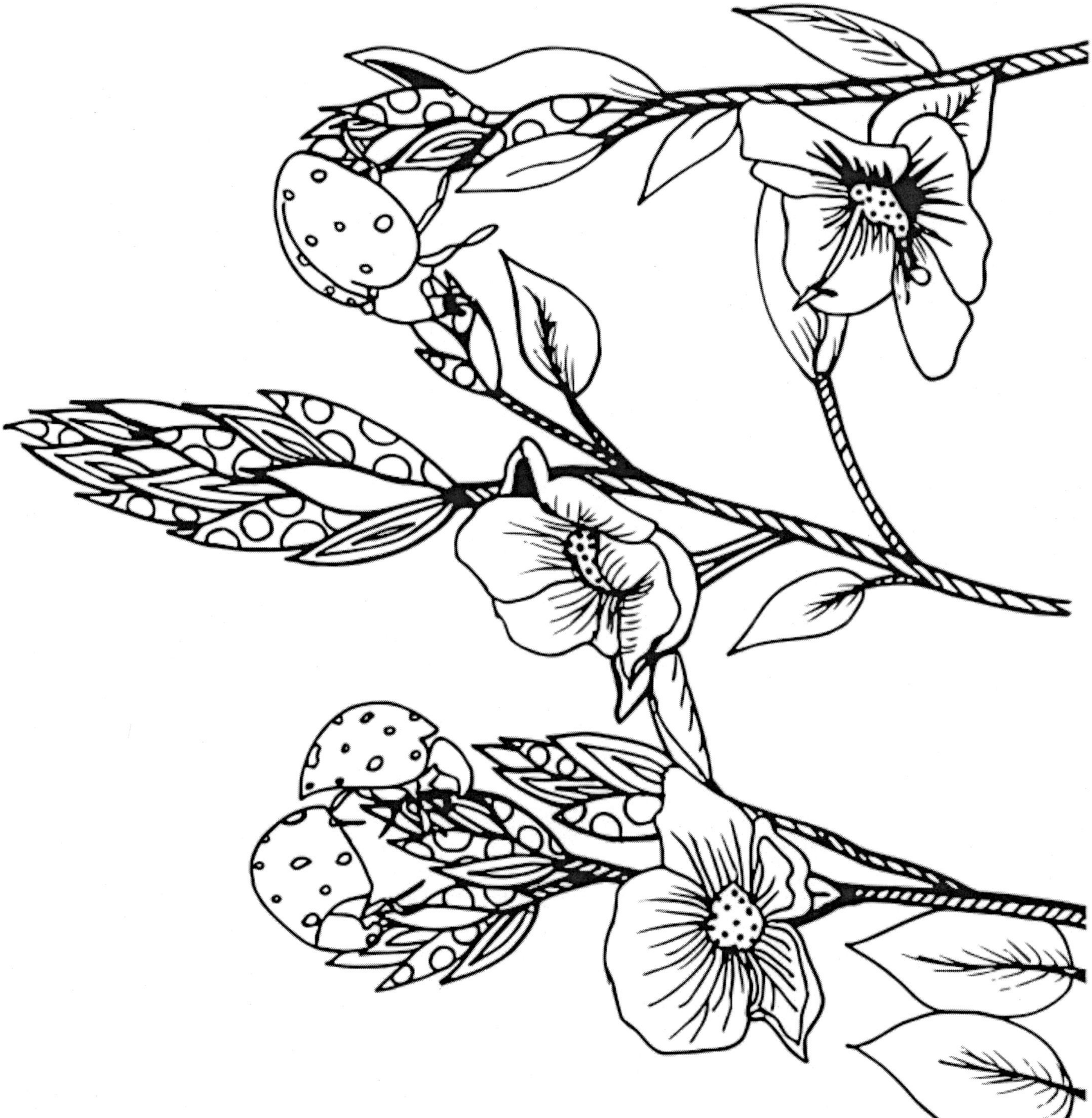

Snail

- **Fun Facts**
    - Snails are nocturnal hermaphrodites. They are also deaf.
    - Snails can lift up to 10 times their own body weight in a vertical position.
    - Snails are sensitive to bright sunlight, which is why they usually show up when it's cloudy out.
    - Garden snails have a top speed of 50 yards per hour. They are one of the slowest creatures on Earth.
    - During winter months and harsh summer droughts, many snails will cover themselves with mucus and hibernate so that they don't dry out.
    - Different species of snails live for drastically different amounts of time. Some only stick around for 5 years or so, while others can live for up to 25.
    - The largest land snail recorded was 12 inches long and weighed nearly 2 pounds.
- **What Do They Eat?**
    - Snails eat a variety of things. One kind—the Giant African Land Snail—eats up to 500 types of plants.
- **Where They Hang Out**
    - There are thousands of species of snails and they can be found all over the world.
- **Helpful Organization**
    - Hawaiian Tree Snail Conservation Lab

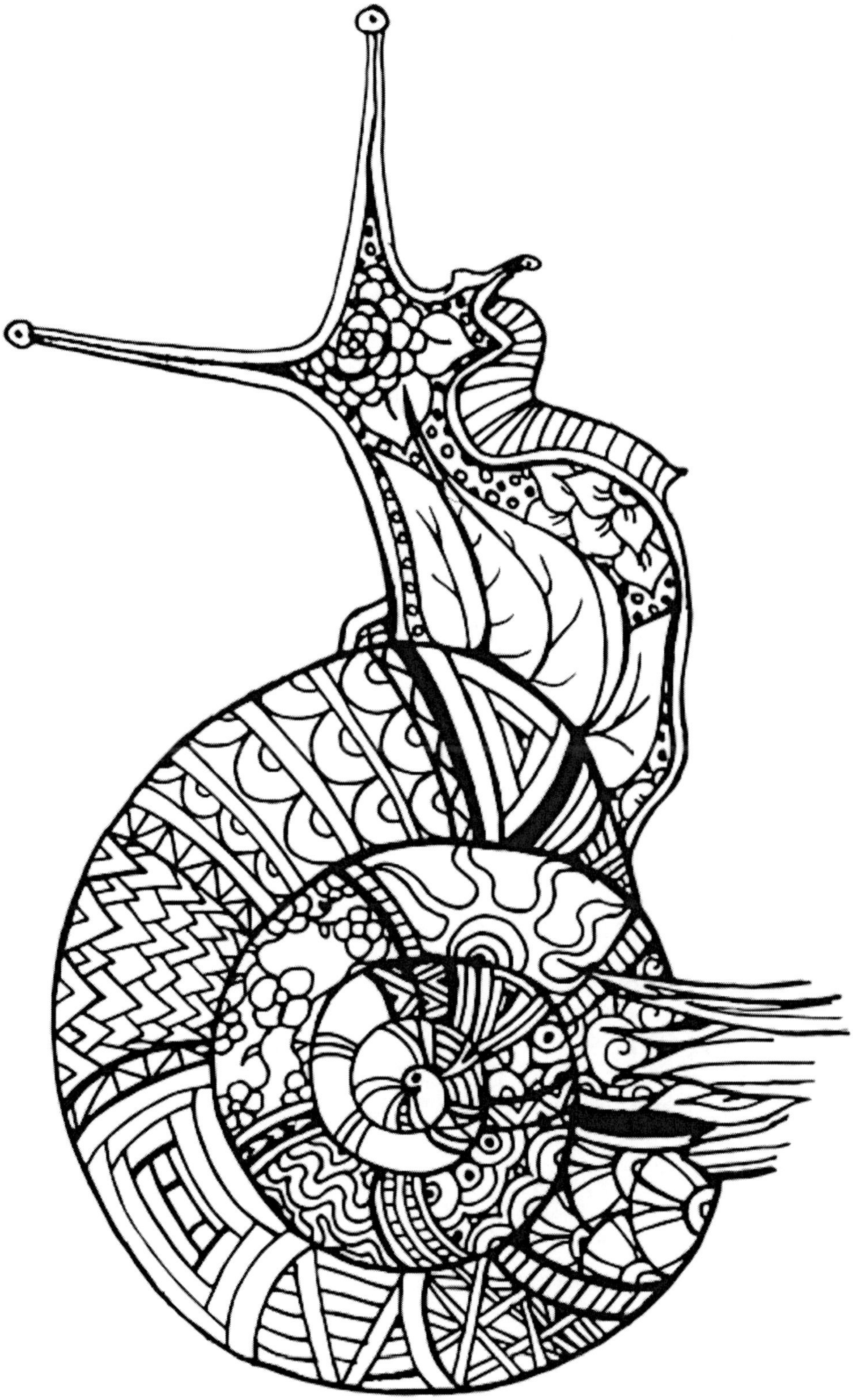

Spider

- **Fun Facts**
  - Spiders have eight legs and chelicerae with fangs that inject venom. Spiders do not have antennae.
  - As of 2015, at least 45,709 spider species have been recorded, and only about 50% of them make webs.
  - Scientists are currently researching spider venom in the interest of creating pain killers, medicines and non-polluting pesticides.
  - Male spiders have to come up with complex courting rituals in order to avoid being eaten by the females. Few of them survive. Female spiders weave silk egg-cases that can house hundreds of eggs at a time.
  - Spider webs are made of many different kinds of silk; each type used has a property like toughness, flexibility, stickiness, etc.
- **What Do tTey Eat?**
  - With the exception of the herbivorous species, *Bagheera kiplingi,* all other spiders are predators that eat insects, birds, and lizards, (depending on their comparative size). They detect their prey by sensing vibrations.
- **Where They Hang Out**
  - Spiders can be found all over the world, with the exception of Antarctica.
- **Helpful Organization**
  - Anthorpe Nature Conservancy Preserve

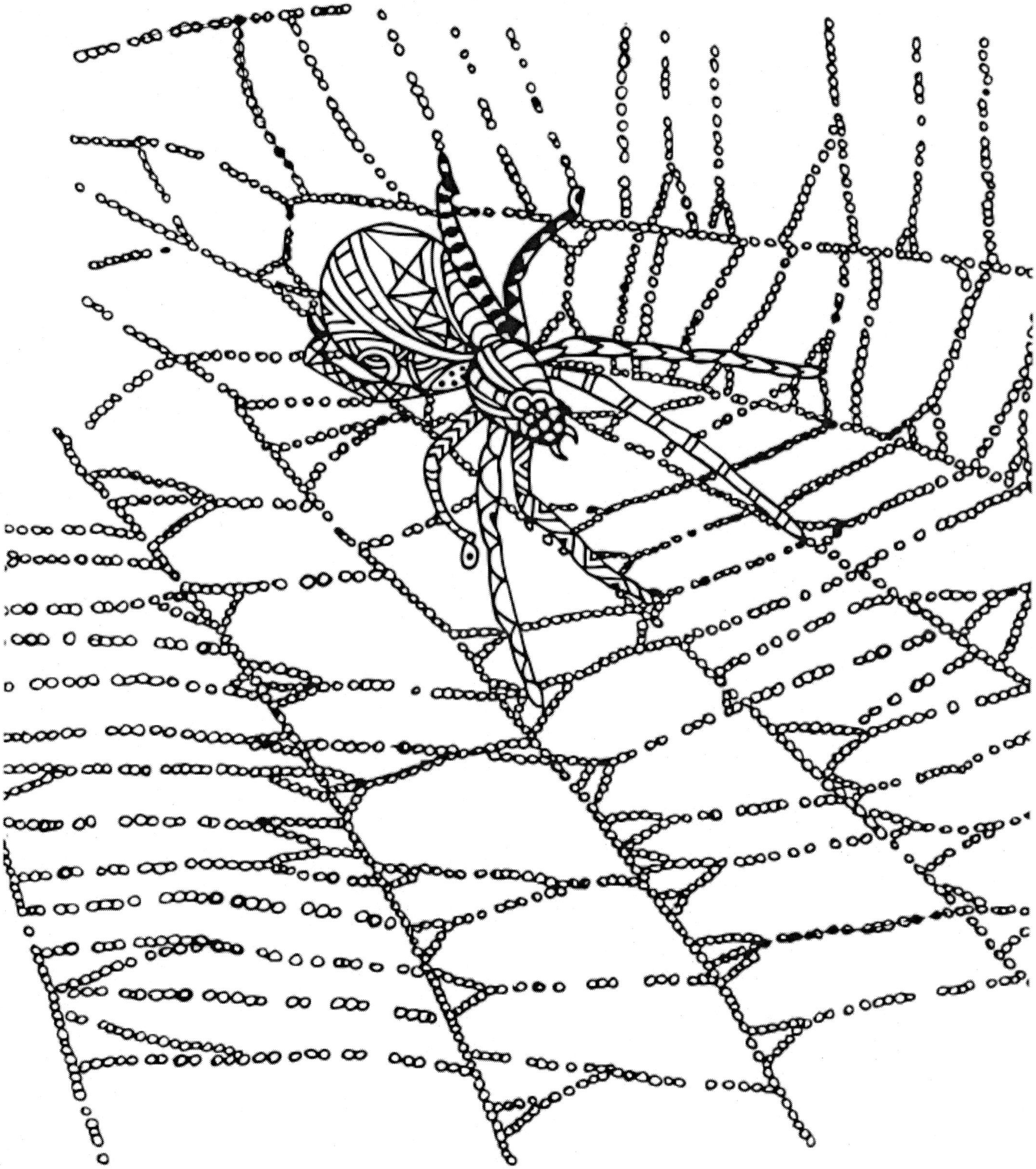

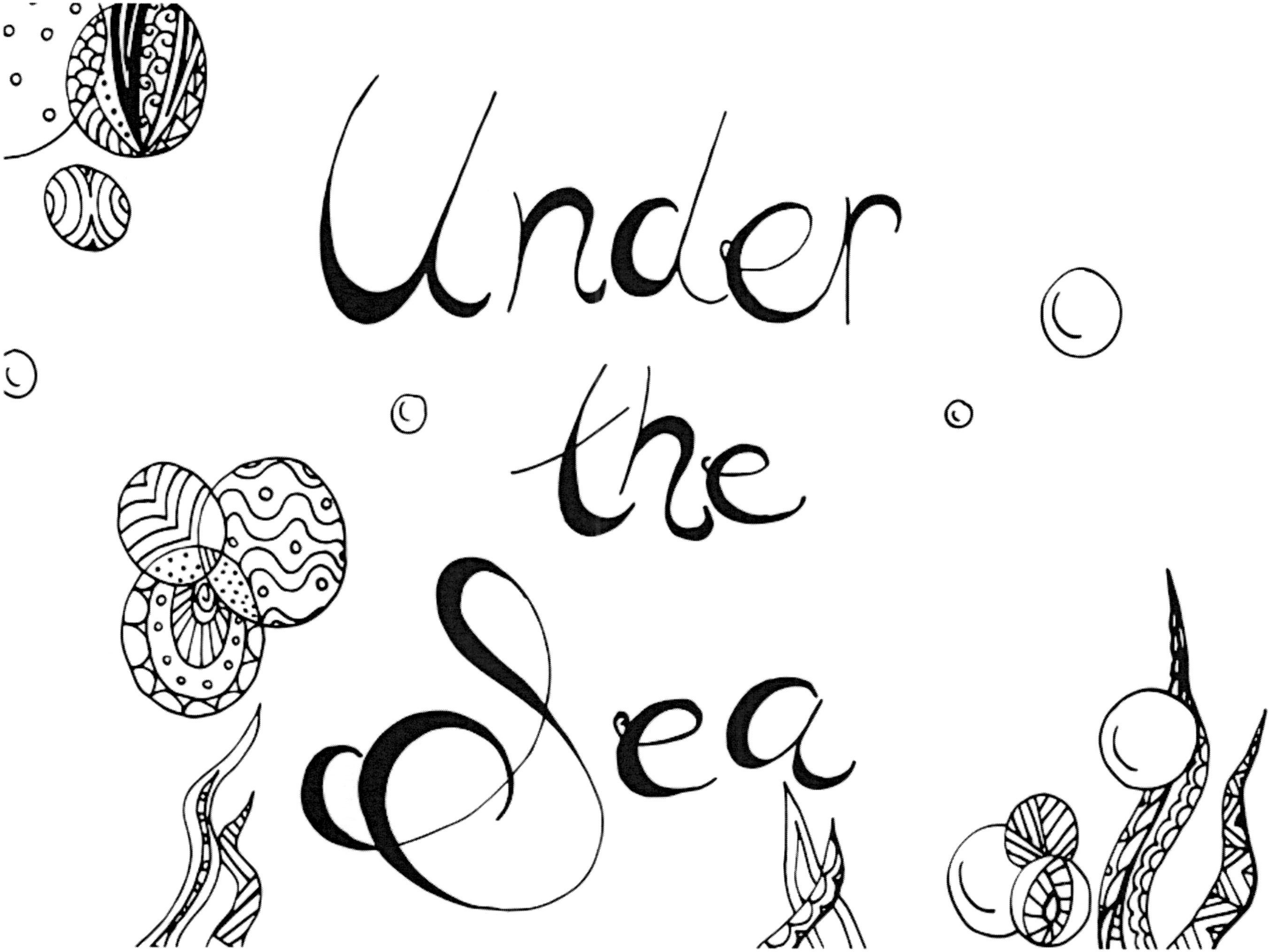
Under the Sea

Seahorse

- **Fun Facts**
  - Seahorses fantastic eyesight. Because their eyes work independent of one another, they are able to look forwards and backwards at the same time.
  - Seahorses keep their mates for life, meeting one another first thing in the morning to reestablish their bond.
  - The male seahorses is the one who becomes pregnant, as the female transfers her eggs to him during mating.
  - Seahorses suck their food in through their snout in much the same fashion as a vacuum cleaner
  - Seahorses have an elaborate mating ritual that spans the course of an hour, during which they will often spiral around an object. During this time, the female enters the male's territory and then returns to her own after it's over. When they first see one another, they change color.
- **What Do They Eat?**
  - Seahorses eat small Mysis shrimp and other small crustaceans.
- **Where They Hang Out**
  - Seahorses stay in shallow, weeded areas during the spring and summer. In the winter, they dive into deeper water.
- **Helpful Organizations**
  - The Seahorse Trust
  - Project Seahorse

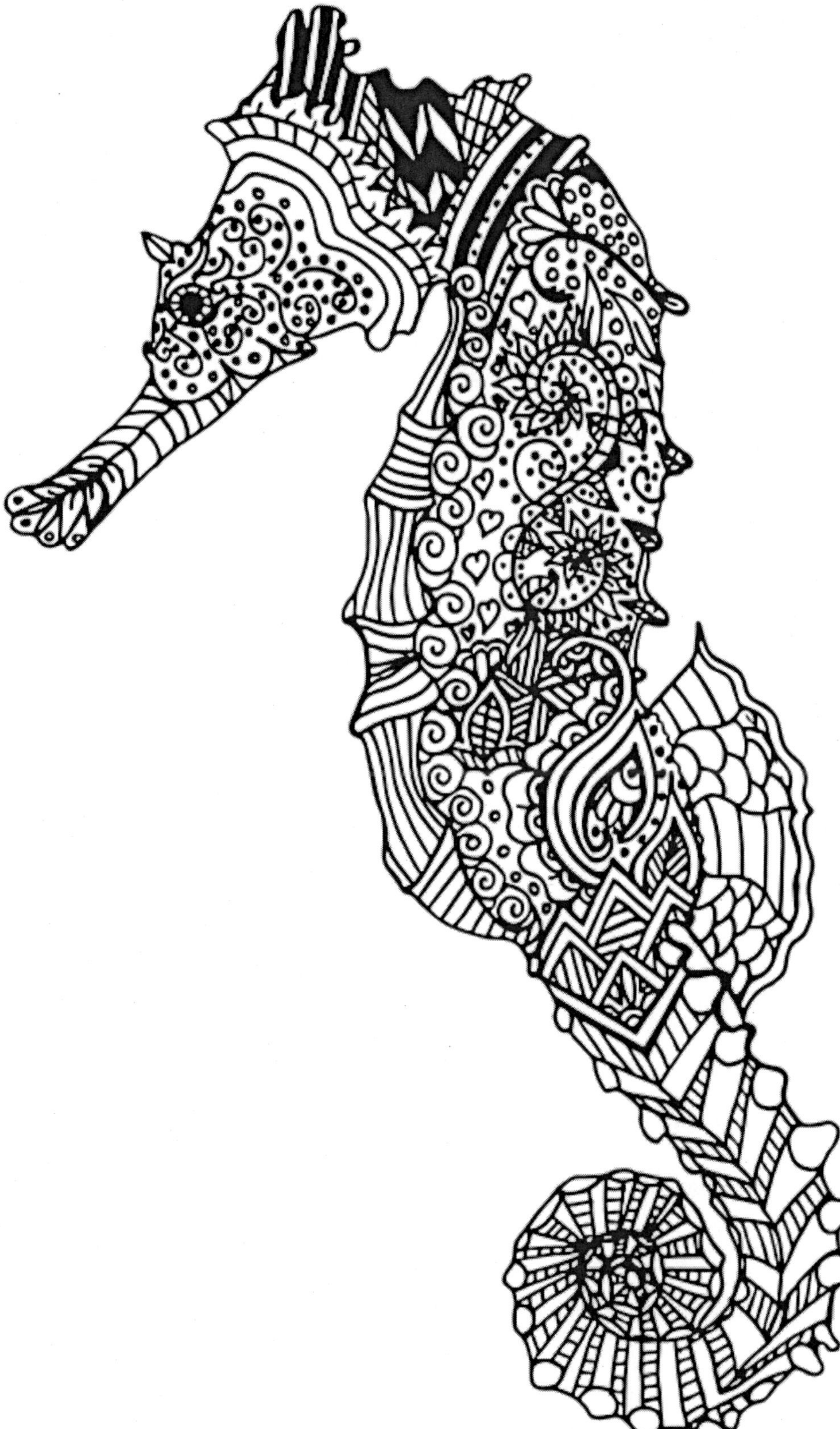

Great White Shark

- **Fun Facts**
  - While up to ½ of the 100+ annual shark attacks are attributable to Great White Sharks, new research is finding that most of these are not fatal, as the sharks habitually "sample bite" their victims and then release them. They actually don't really enjoy eating humans at all and often mistake them for other fish, (especially surfers, whose boards mimic the shapes of many aquatic creatures that sharks actually *like* to eat, like beluga whales).
  - Great White Sharks grow to be an average of 15' long and can weigh up to 5k lbs.
  - Great Whites have up to 300 serrated, triangular teeth that are arranged in several rows along their mouths.
  - Great White Sharks are on the "endangered" list due to over-fishing and accidental catching in grill nets.
  - Great White Sharks can detect 1 single drop of blood in up to 25 gallons of water 3 miles away.
- **What Do They Eat?**
  - Young Great Whites eat fish and rays, while adults eat small-toothed whales, otters, and sea turtles.
- **Where They Hang Out**
  - Great White Sharks prefer cool, coastal waters.
- **Helpful Organizations**
  - Atlantic White Shark Conservancy
  - The Great White Shark Project

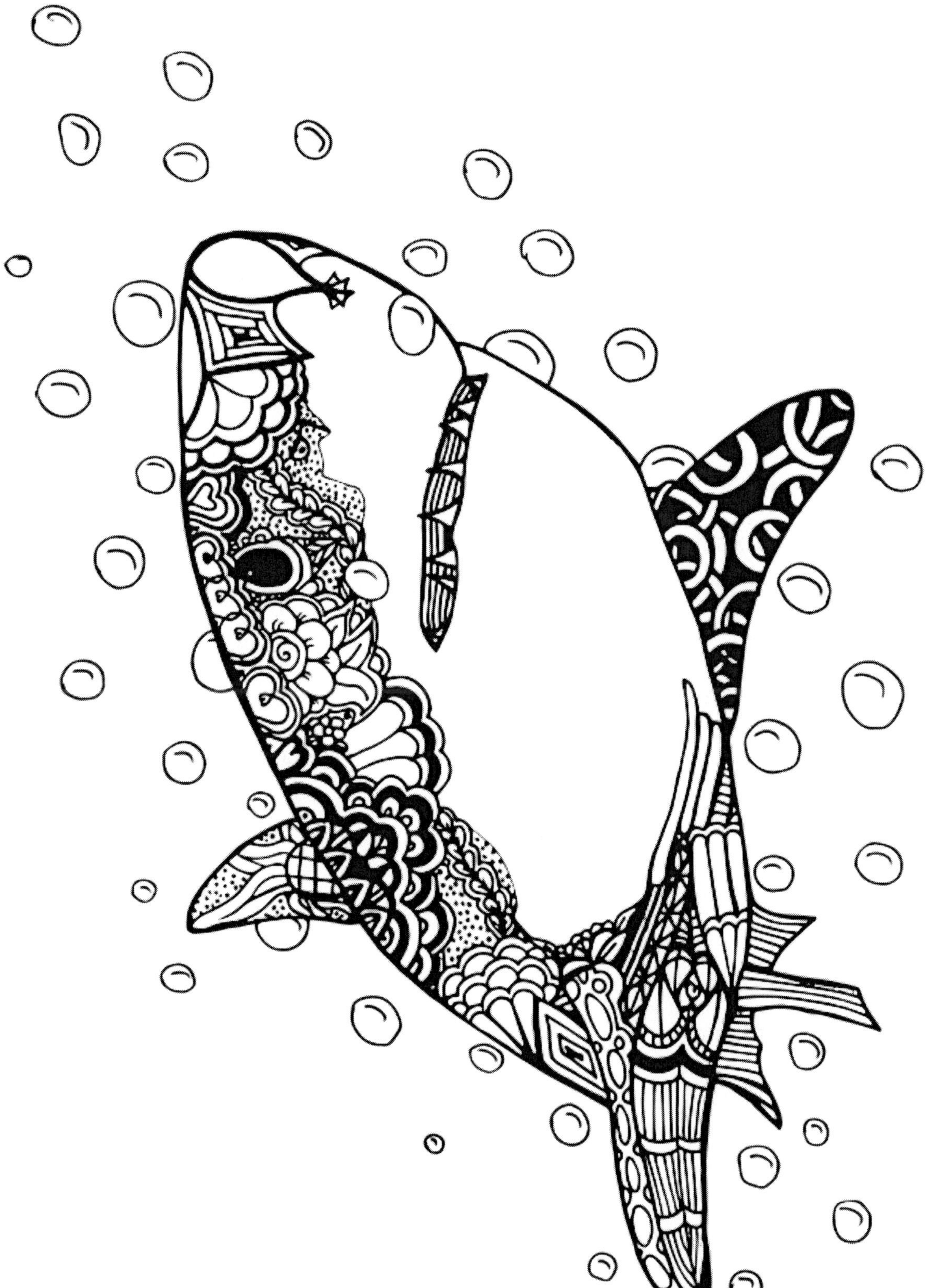

Manatee

- **Fun Facts**
  - Manatees can consume up to 15% of their body weight in vegetation daily
  - The average adult manatee is about 10' long and can weigh up to 12k lbs.
  - Manatees can “sprint” up to 20 mph for very short periods of time, but they average 3-4 mph
  - Manatees can live to be up to 60 years old.
  - Manatees are mammals and must surface to breathe air every 3-5 minutes.
  - The manatee's closest “relative” in the animal world is the elephant.
  - Manatees really don't have very many natural enemies. They are most threatened by an increasing loss of habitat and by collisions with watercraft. That's why it's incredibly important to look out for them while boating.
- **What Do They Eat?**
  - Manatees are herbivores, eating mostly floating plants
- **Where They Hang Out**
  - Manatees stay in estuaries, saltwater bays, canals, coastal areas, and slow-moving rivers.
- **Helpful Organizations**
  - Save the Manatee Club
  - Adopt-A-Manatee

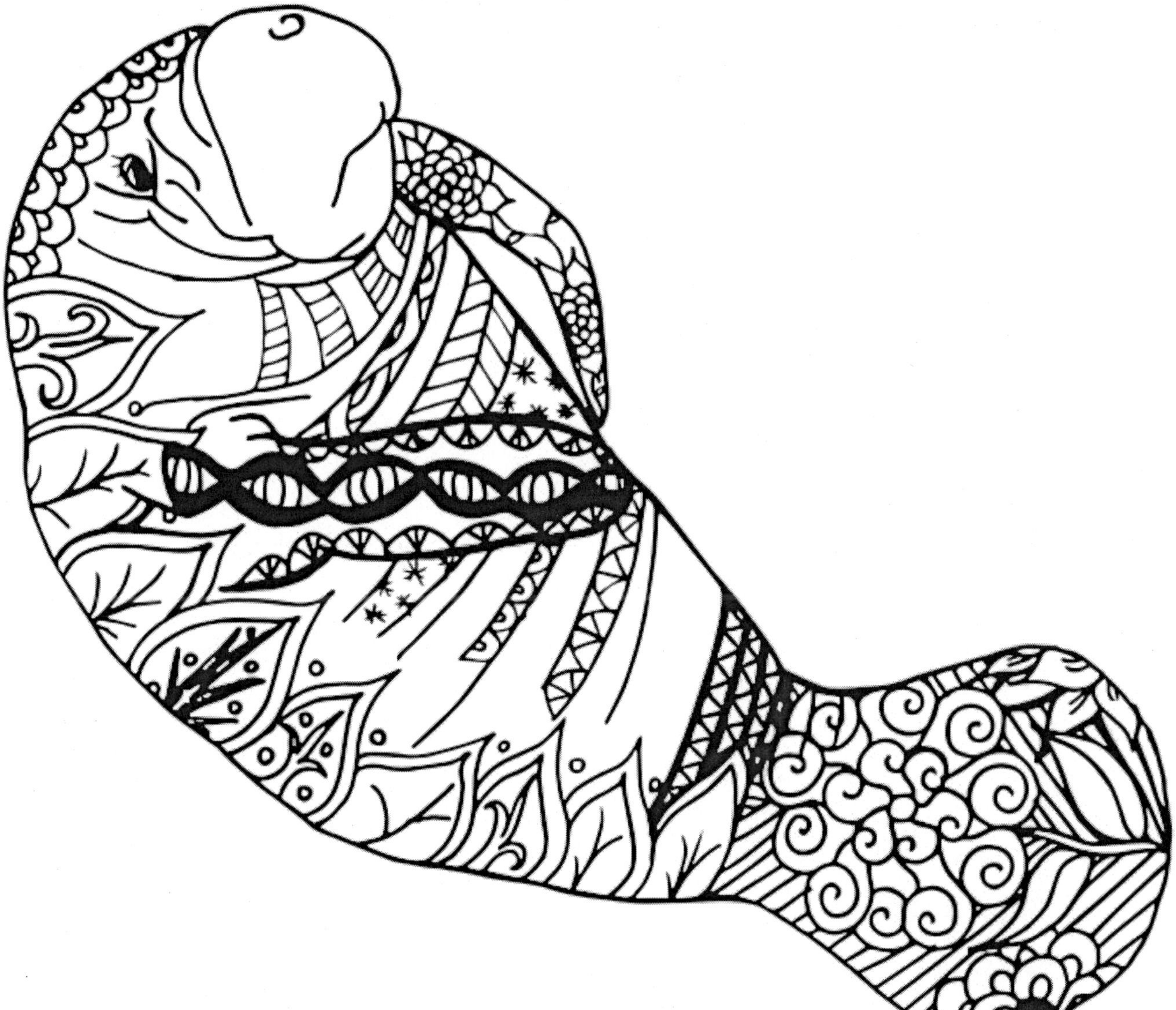

Sea Lion

- **Fun Facts**
  - Sea lions only have two natural predators: Orca "Killer" Whales and Sharks. Despite this, they are still considered endangered. This mainly has to do with environmental issues.
  - Sea lions are very social. They live in large colonies and stay close together for protection.
  - Sea Lions can live up to 20-30 years in the wild.
  - Sea Lions can handle colder temperatures because of a thick, insulating later of blubber that coats their bodies
  - Ancestral Sea Lions used to live on land.
  - Sea Lions can rotate their rear flippers to face forward, allowing them to walk around on land fairly well.
- **What To They Eat?**
  - Sea Lions are carnivorous, feasting mostly on fish, squid, and shellfish
- **Where They Hang Out**
  - Geographically, you can find sea lions almost everywhere, though their numbers are dwindling down. The largest sea lion can be seen in the Northern Pacific—particularly in Alaska.
- **Helpful Organization**
  - The Seal Conservation Society

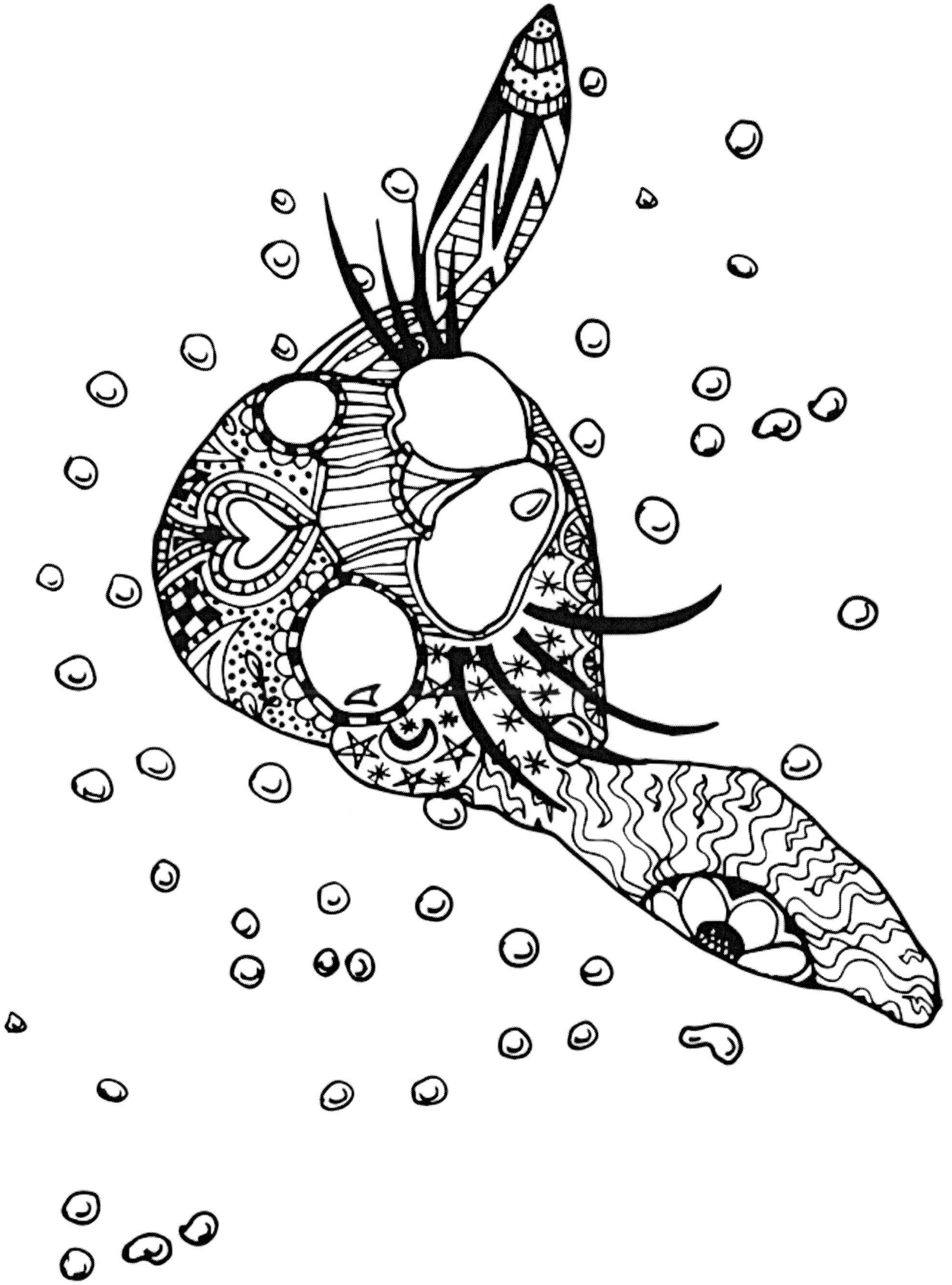

Beluga Whale

- **Fun Facts**
  - The beluga whale can swim backwards.
  - Beluga whales are able to change the shape of their heads by blowing air around their sinuses
  - Beluga whales do not have dorsal fins. They instead have a dorsal ridge. This helps them withstand arctic temperatures because dorsal fins actually cause extra heat loss.
  - A beluga can turn its head up, down, and side-to-side because the vertebrae in its neck are not fused together.
  - Belugas can dive down up to 800 meters and stay under the water for up to 25 minutes.
  - Beluga whales are one of the smallest and most vocal whales in the world
  - If a female loses her calf, she will carry planks, and buoys around during calving season. It's thought that they use these items as calf surrogates.
- **What Do They Eat?**
  - Beluga whales eat fish, krill, squid, crabs, crustaceans, octopus, and sand worms.
- **Where They Hang Out**
  - Beluga whales live in the Arctic and Subarctic waters near Russia, North America, and Greenland.
- **Helpful Organization**
  - Beluga Whale Management and Recovery

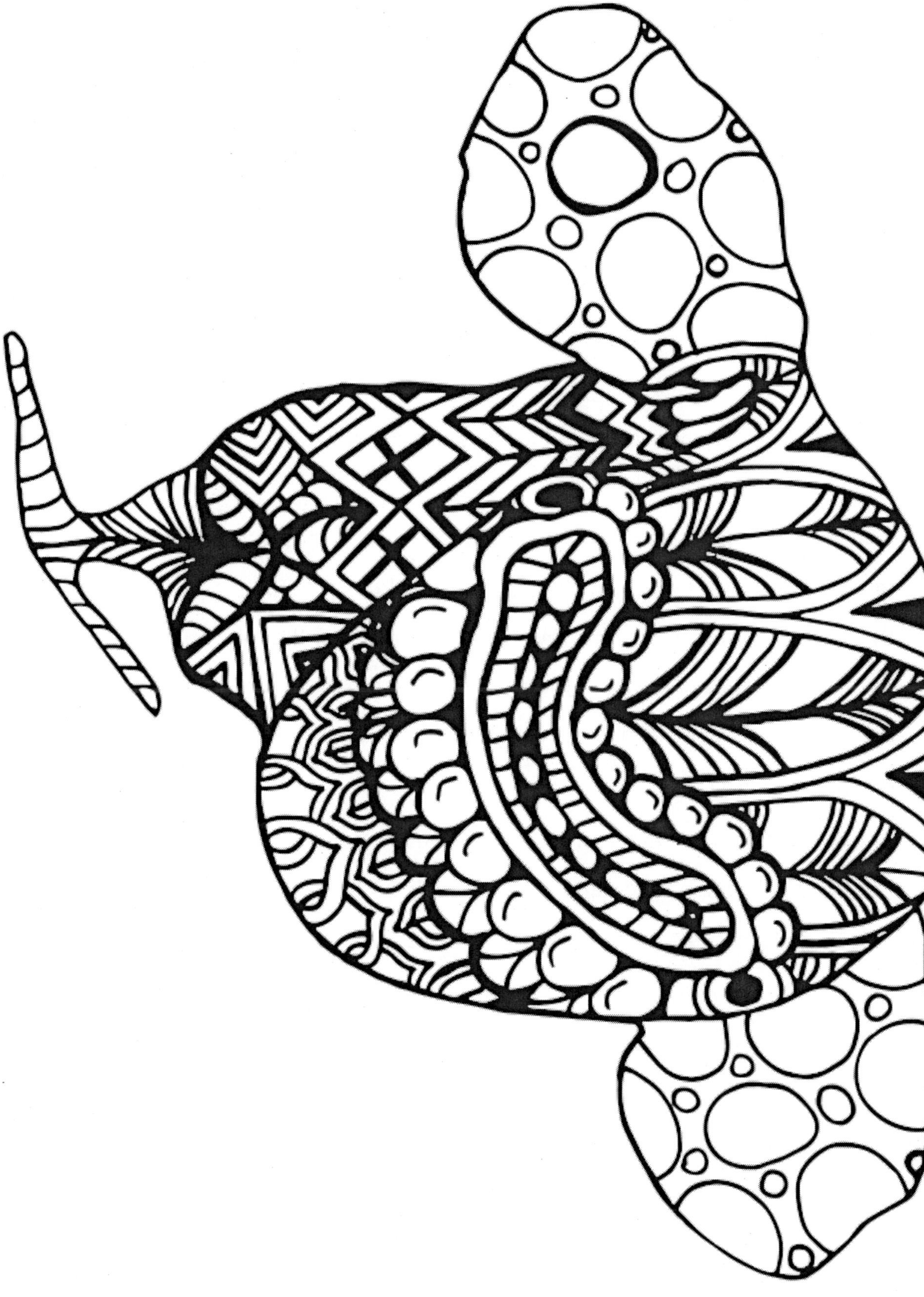

Bottle-Nose Dolphins

- **Fun Facts**
  - Bottle-Nose dolphins cooperate together to survive. They form complex hunting teams to get food and have a midwife system for raising their young.
  - Bottle-Nose dolphins are able to make calls that are so loud that they stun fish. This helps them hunt. They will also flip a fish out of the water, shocking them into a sort of paralysis.
  - Bottle-Nose dolphins are warm-blooded and can stay under water for up to 15 minutes.
  - Bottle-Nose dolphins have compartmentalized stomachs that help them digest their food efficiently.
  - Bottle-Nose dolphins do not chew their food. Instead, they will shake them or rub them on the ocean floor until their prey breaks apart into smaller pieces. They also strip meat from spiny fishes to avoid injury from the spines.
- **What Do They Eat?**
  - Bottle-Nose dolphins eat fish, squid, and crustaceans. They eat between 4-6% of their body weight in food daily.
- **Where They Hang Out**
  - Bottle-Nose dolphins can be found throughout the Pacific and Atlantic. They generally stay between Norway and the tip of Africa and between Japan and Australia. They don't generally go anywhere north or south of those areas.
- **Helpful Organization**
  - The Dolphin Institute

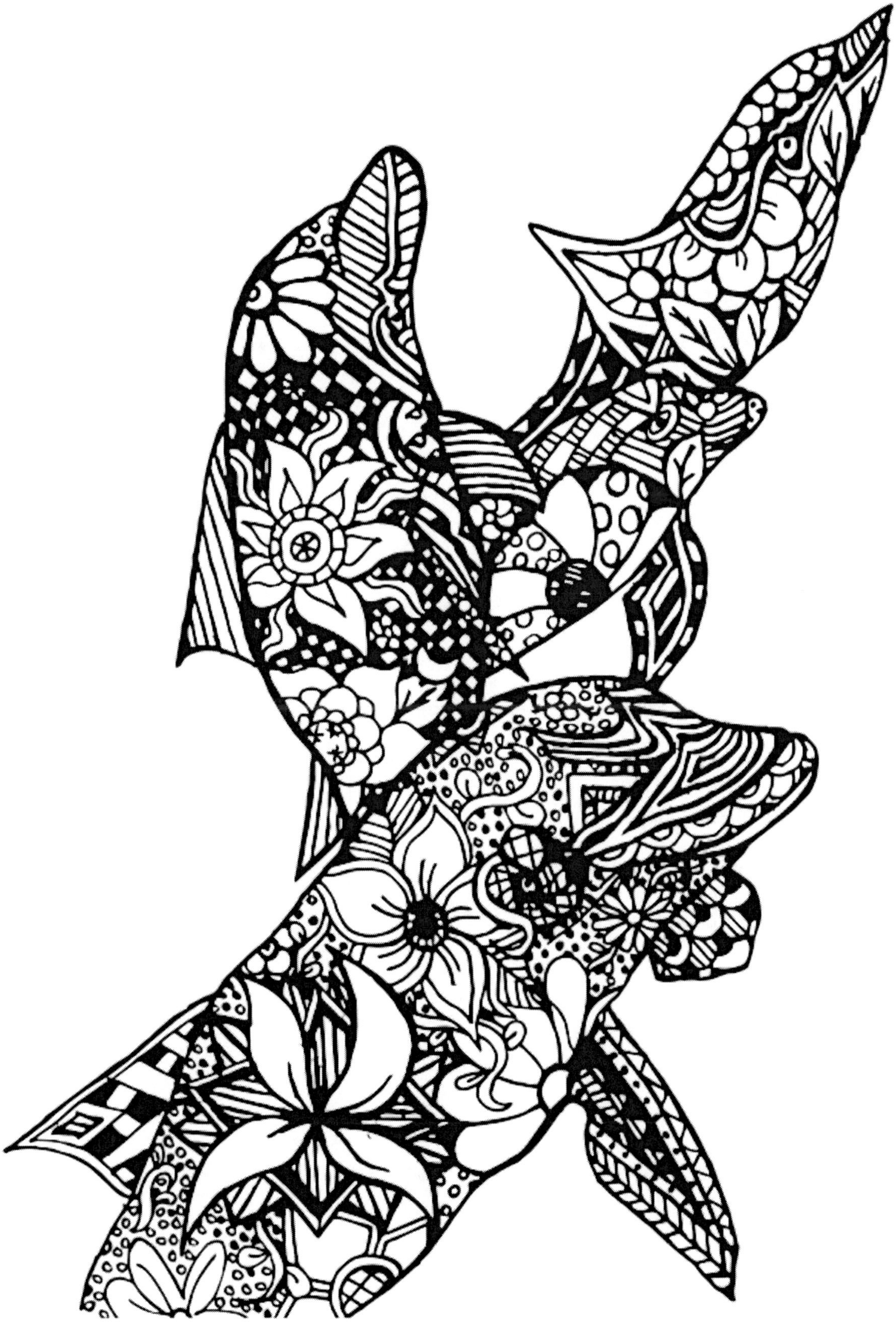

Orca

- **Fun Facts**
  - Orcas area also known as Killer Whales and are the largest dolphins in the world
  - Orcas travel in pods that act as cooperative hunting teams similar to wolf packs.
  - Orcas have distinctive noises that each member of their pod can recognize at great distances. This helps them communicate while they are hunting and traveling. They also use echolocation to determine how far they are from their prey and from one another.
  - Orcas are protective of their young and even employ a nanny system to ensure that they are cared for.
  - Orcas give birth every 3-10 years and their pregnancies last up to 17 months.
- **What Do They Eat?**
  - Orcas eat seals, sea lions, and even smaller whales. They are fierce predators and have been known to grab seals right off of the ice in one single swoop.
- **Where They Hang Out**
  - Orcas prefer cold, coastal waters, although they can be seen everywhere from the poles to the equator.
- **Helpful Organizations**
  - Center for Whale Research
  - Orca Conservancy

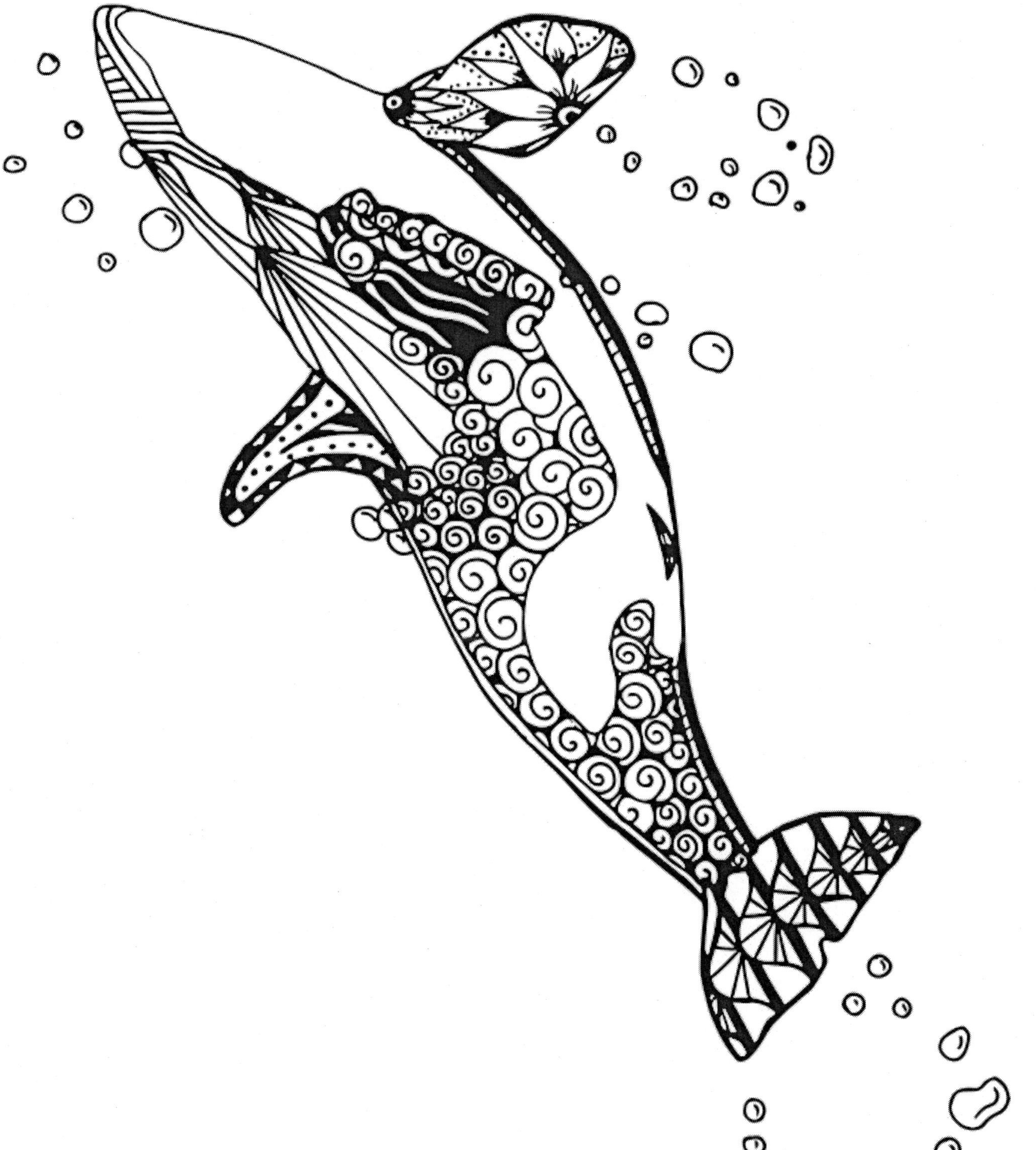

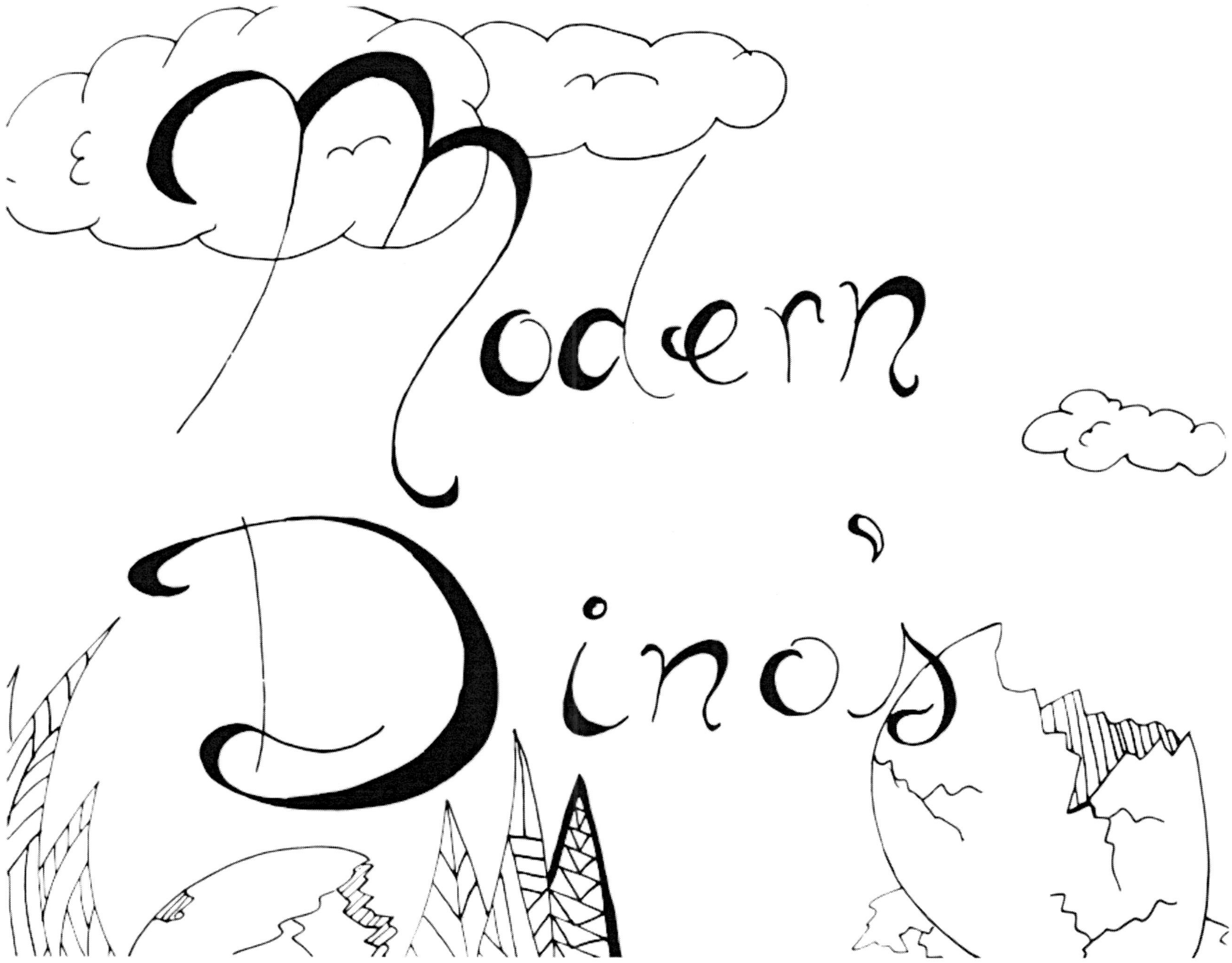
Modern
Dino's

Sea Turtle

- **Fun Facts**
  - Six of the seven species of sea turtles are considered threatened or endangered.
  - Smaller sea turtles weigh between 80-100 lbs, while the larger turtles, (like the Leatherback Sea Turtle), can weigh more than 1,000 lbs.
  - Sea Turtles spend their entire lives in the ocean. The only exception to this rule is when a female comes ashore to lay her eggs.
  - When sea turtles hatch, they look for the reflections along the water to determine what direction to crawl towards. In highly developed seaside towns, night time lights can cause confusion and they will walk in the wrong direction. This is particularly problematic and is one of the reasons their numbers are declining.
- **What Do They Eat?**
  - Some eat sea grasses, while others eat sponges, crabs, clams, and jellyfish. It all depends on their species.
- **Where They Hang Out**
  - Sea Turtles can be found throughout the world, so long as there is an ocean for them to swim in. They prefer tropical and subtropical regions, but the Leatherback Sea Turtle has been seen in colder temperatures in the northern regions of Alaska.
- **Helpful Organizations**
  - Sea Turtle Conservancy

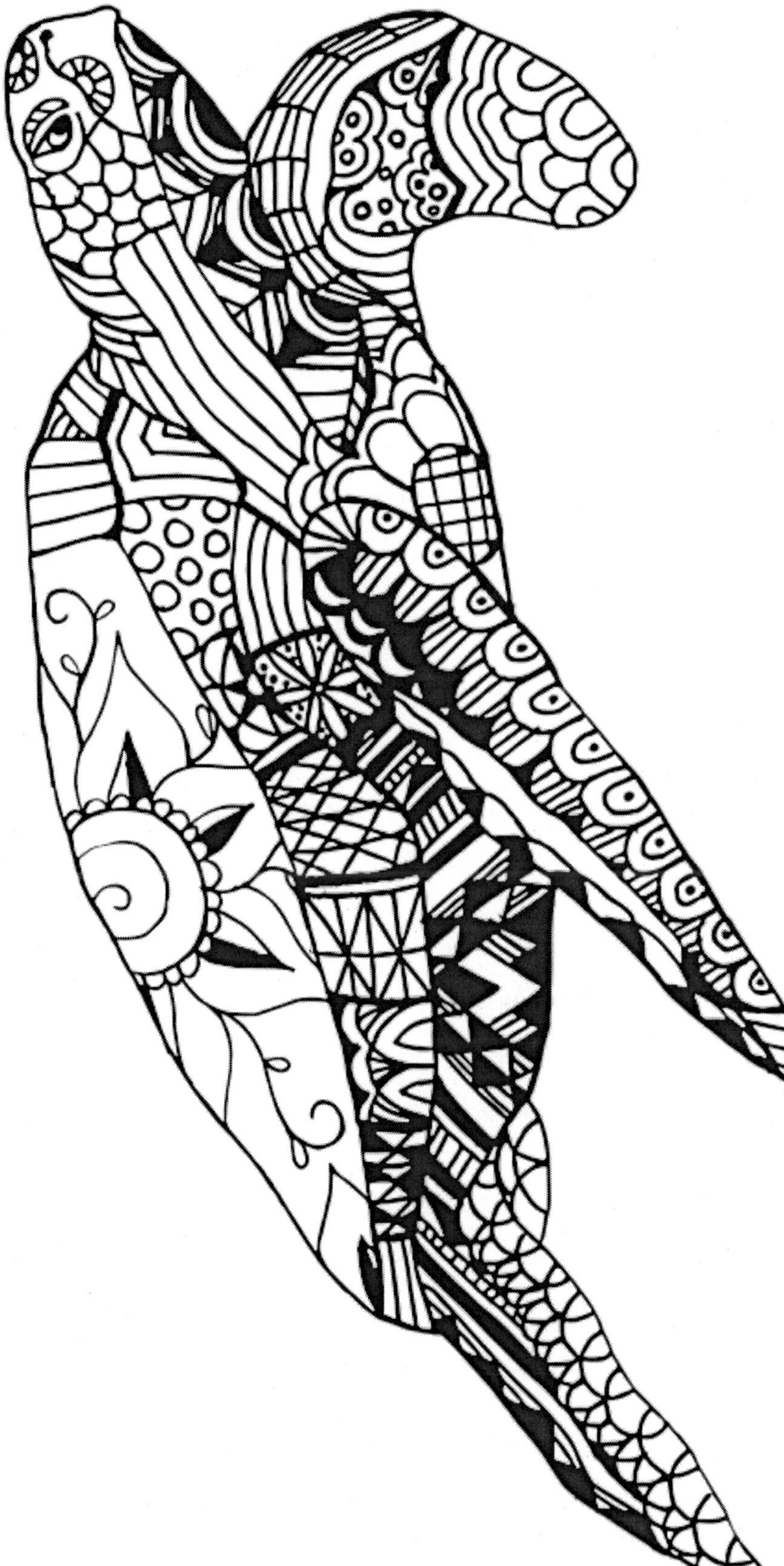

Alligator

- **Fun Facts**
  - Unlike crocodiles, when an alligator closes its mouth, all of its upper teeth can still be seen.
  - There are two different types of alligators: The American Alligator and Chinese Alligators. American Alligators can grow up to 11.2 feet long and weigh close to a full ton. Chinese Alligators grow up to 4.9 feet long and weigh around 50 lbs.
  - Alligators are very social. They live in large groups called congregations.
  - Alligators have a difficult time controlling their temperature on their own. It is for that reason that they are often seen sunning themselves on banks or cooling off in lakes.
  - Alligators are awkward on land, but in the water they are swift. They can swim up to 20 mph.
- **What Do They Eat?**
  - Alligators are carnivorous creatures. They will eat small mammals, birds, fish, and mollusks. Sometimes they will also snack on fruit, though it's not their meal of choice.
- **Where They Hang Out**
  - The American Alligator can be found throughout the southern half of the United States. Chinese Alligators live throughout Eastern China, particularly close to the Pacific Ocean and the Yangtze River.
- **Helpful Organizations**
  - National Parks Conservation Association

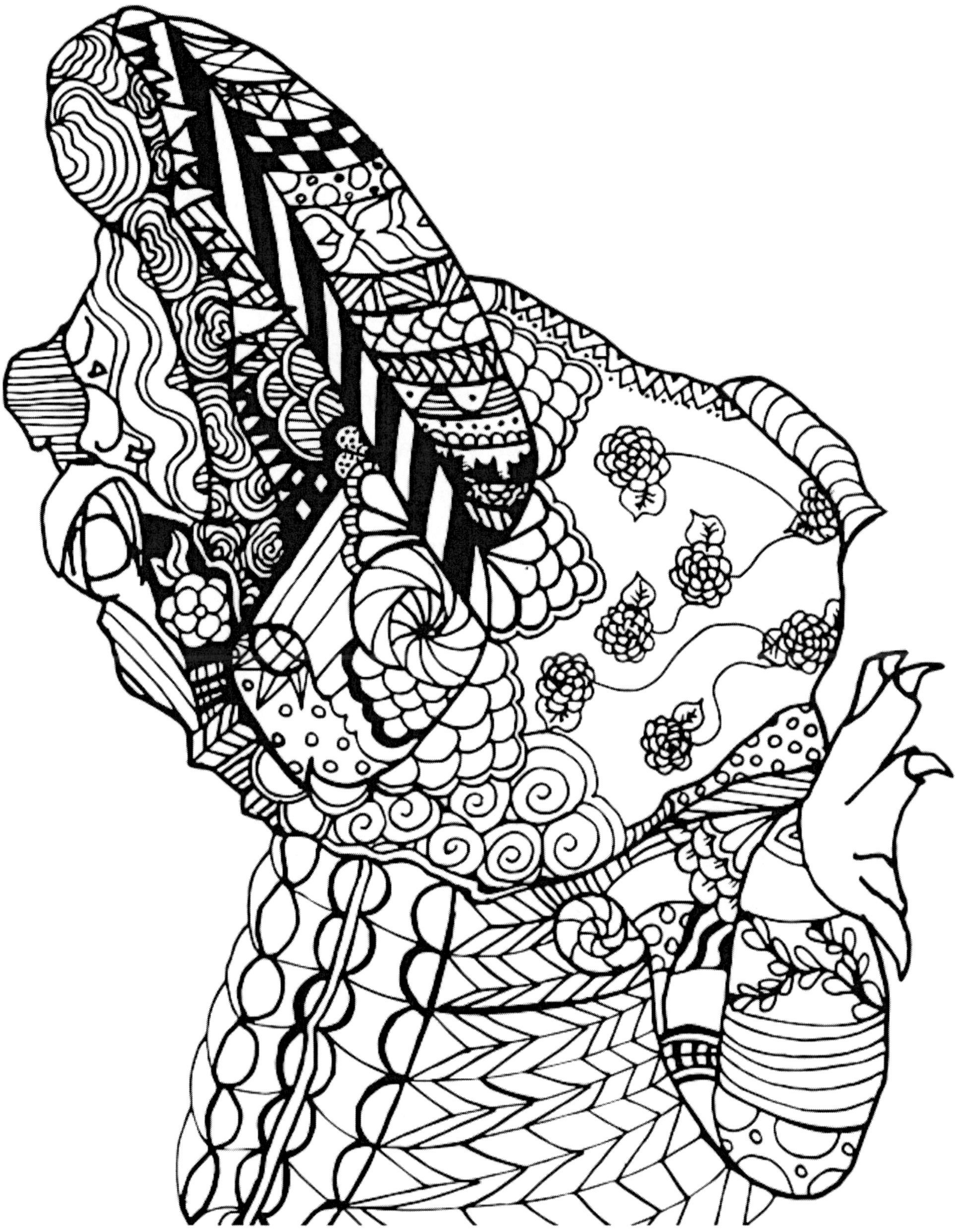

Chameleon

- **Fun Facts**
    - Unlike most animals in the wild, chameleons continue to grow larger and larger throughout their lives. To keep up with their growth rate, they shed small pieces of their skin at a time.
    - Chameleons change colors in response to temperature changes, humidity, as a camouflage technique, to show emotion, and to communicate with one another.
    - The brighter a chameleon's color, the more dominant the male is. This is similar to how a peacock shows off its feathers to attract a mate and intimidate its rivals.
    - Chameleons can move their eyes independently of one another, giving them a nearly full 360-degree view of their surroundings. They can also focus and enlarge what they are looking at. In that way, their eyes sort of act like a camera lens.
- **What Do They Eat?**
    - Chameleons eat small birds and insects. They have strong stomach acids that aid in digestion.
- **Where They Hang Out**
    - You can find wild chameleons throughout Africa, Spain, Portugal, and Asia. They have also been seen in Madagascar. They tend to prefer rainforests and savannahs.
- **Helpful Organization**
    - The Darwin Initiative

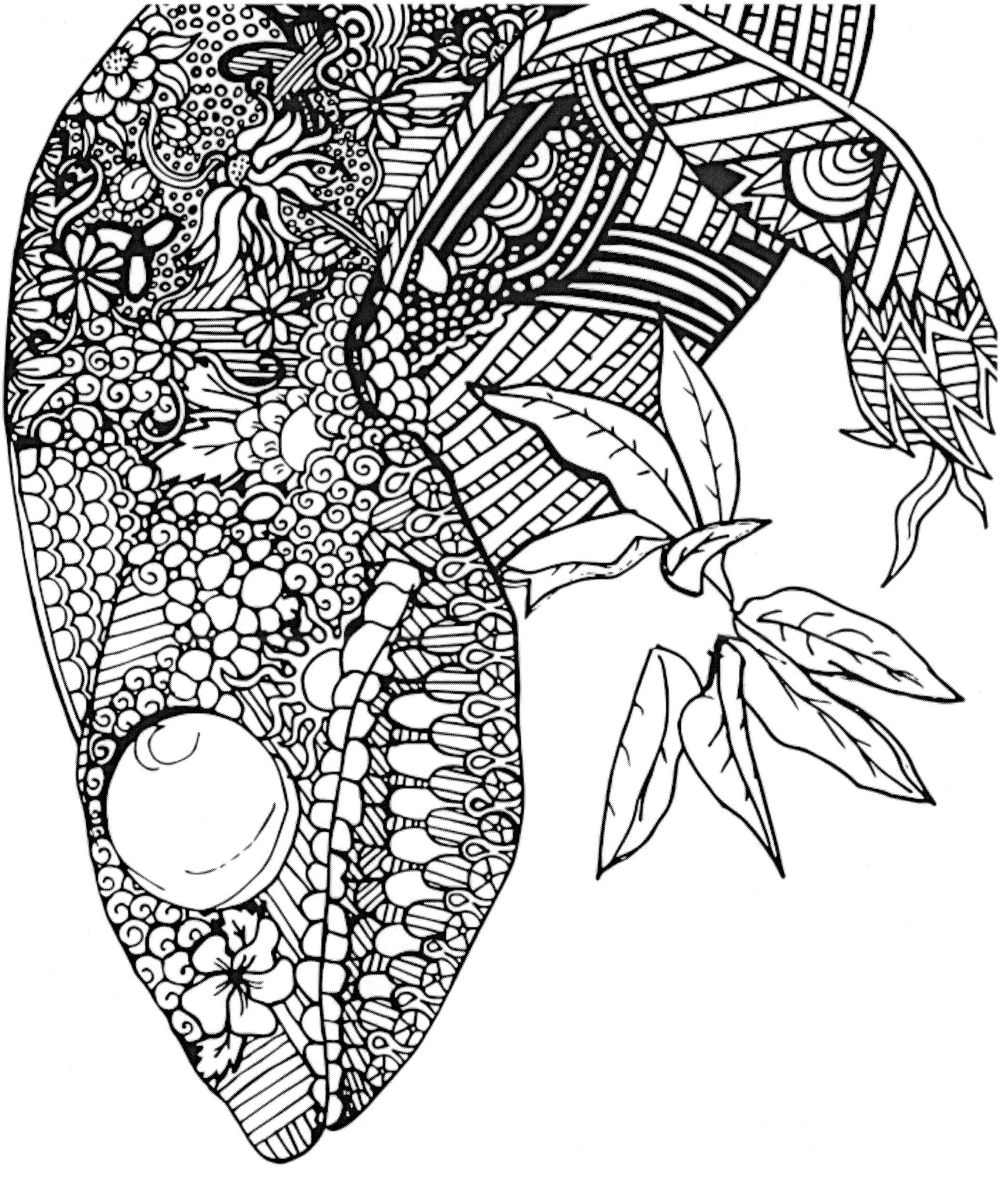

Rhinoceros Iguana

- **Fun Facts**
  - Rhinoceros iguanas are covered in scales that range from a brownish gray color to olive green.
  - Male rhino iguanas are very territorial creatures.
  - Rhino iguanas can live up to 20 years in captivity.
  - Female rhino iguanas lay between 2-20 eggs at a time. Babies are independent from the moment they're born.
  - Unlike frogs, rhino iguanas start off carnivorous and then become herbivorous once they reach adulthood.
  - Rhinoceros iguanas get their name from the small horns atop their heads, which resemble those of a rhinoceros.
  - Female rhinoceros iguanas only breed once a year.
  - The rhinoceros iguana in the picture is dedicated to my cousins' pet "baby dino" rhinoceros iguana, Sam.
- **What Do They Eat?**
  - Baby rhino iguanas eat insects. Adult rhinoceros iguanas eat flowers, leaves, berries, and fruit.
- **Where They Hang Out**
  - Rhinoceros iguanas come from Haiti, Cuba, Puerto Rico, and the Dominican Republic. They like dry, rocky, coastal areas and dig burrows beneath trees and shrubs.
- **Helpful Organizations**
  - Iguana Conservation Project

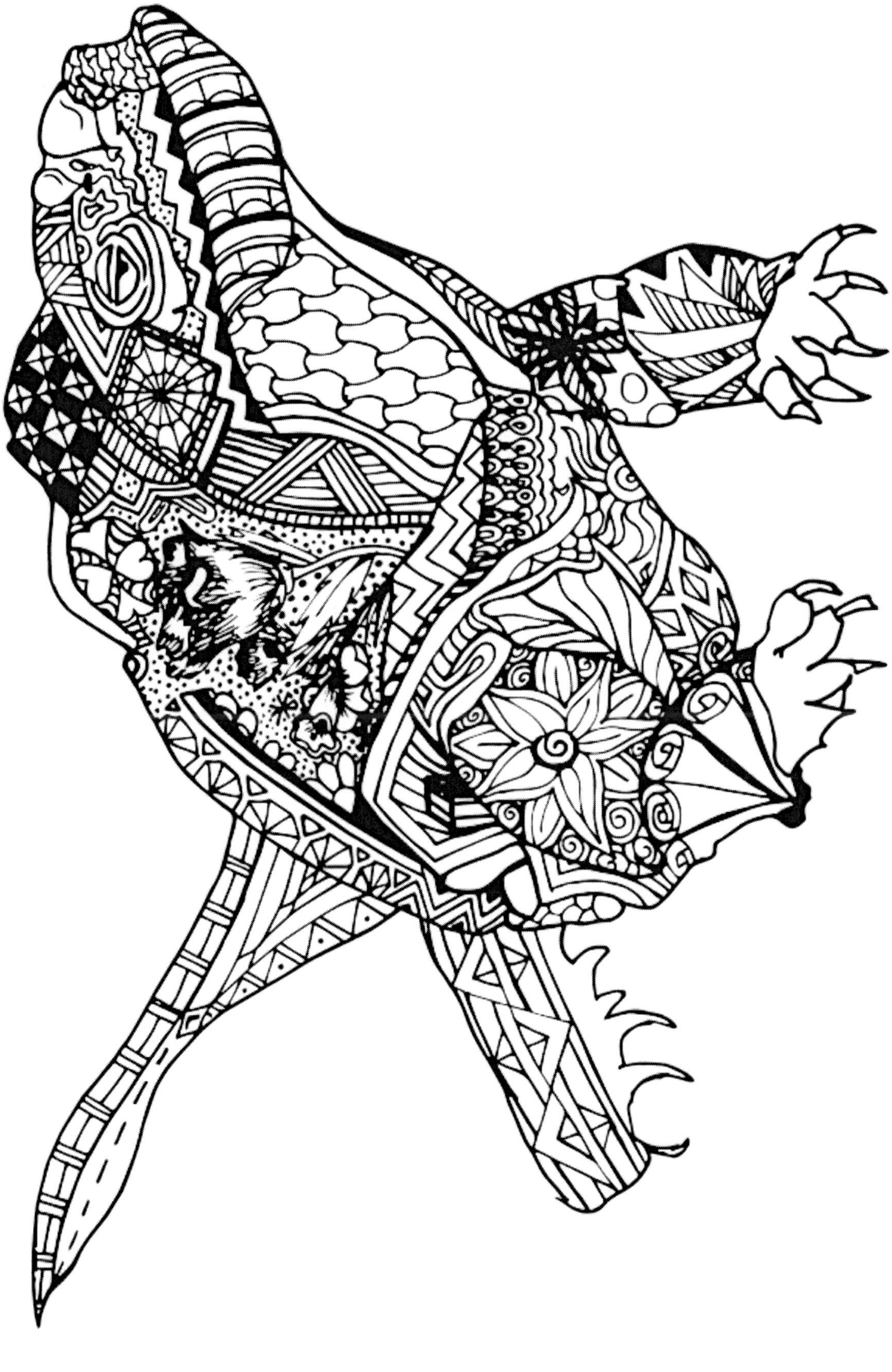

Snake

- **Fun Facts**
  - There are about 2,900 different species of snakes. Of these, only 375 species are venomous.
  - Snakes can consume food more than three times the diameter of their heads because they are able to unhinge their lower jaw.
  - Snakes smell the air by flicking their forked tongues.
  - Snakes have to regulate their body temperatures externally by sunning themselves or retreating to cooler areas.
  - Snakes hibernate during the winter
  - Snakes have to shed their skin between three and six times per year.
- **What Do They Eat?**
  - Snakes are carnivorous creatures that snack on small deer, insects, birds, termites, rodents, frogs, and other reptiles.
- **Where They Hang Out**
  - Snakes are found all over the world, with the exception of Alaska, Iceland, Ireland, Greenland, New Zealand, and Antarctica. This is primarily because they are unable to withstand frigid temperatures. They prefer tropical regions and dry deserts.
- **Helpful Organization**
  - Center for Snake Conservation

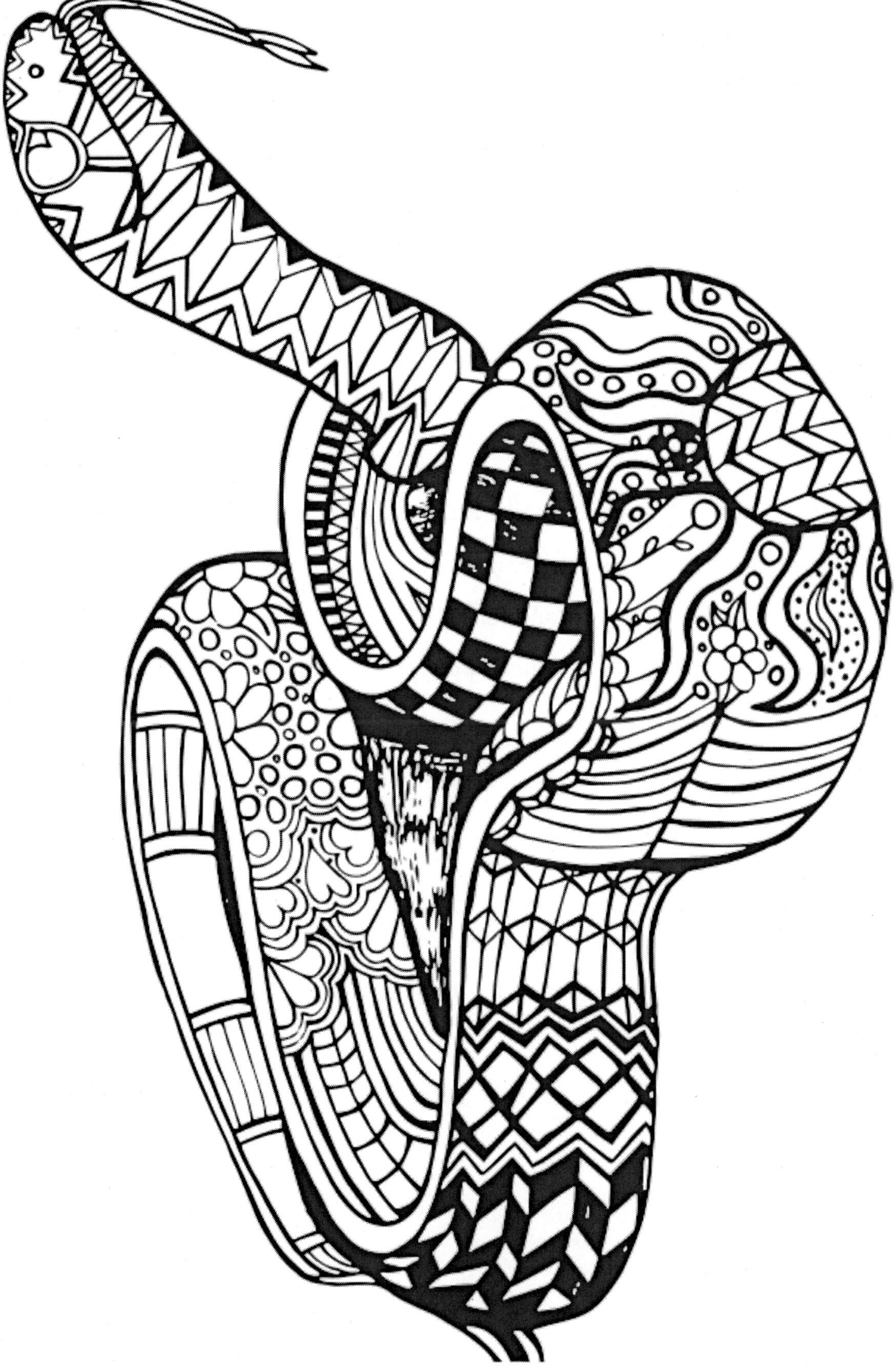

Tree Frog

- **Fun Facts**
  - Tree frogs have rounded suction cups on the bottom of their toes that help them climb high up into trees.
  - The smallest tree frogs in the world fully mature at under an inch long. The largest grow up to about 5-1/2 inches in length.
  - Tree frogs come in a variety of beautiful colors. Some are brown, green, or gray, while others are able to change their colors the way chameleons do.
  - There are over 800 species of tree frogs worldwide.
  - The lifespan of a tree frog depends largely on its species. Some only live for about 3 years, while others stick around for nearly 15. It is estimated that the average lifespan among all of the species is about 5-9 years.
- **What Do They Eat?**
  - As tadpoles, tree frogs are herbivores. As adults, tree frogs mainly eat ants, beetles, crickets, flies, moths, spiders, and small worms.
- **Where They Hang Out**
  - Most tree frogs can be found among the trees of most warmer areas of the world. Some, however, prefer to spend their days in lakes and ponds.
- **Helpful Organization**
  - Amphibian Rescue and Conservation Project

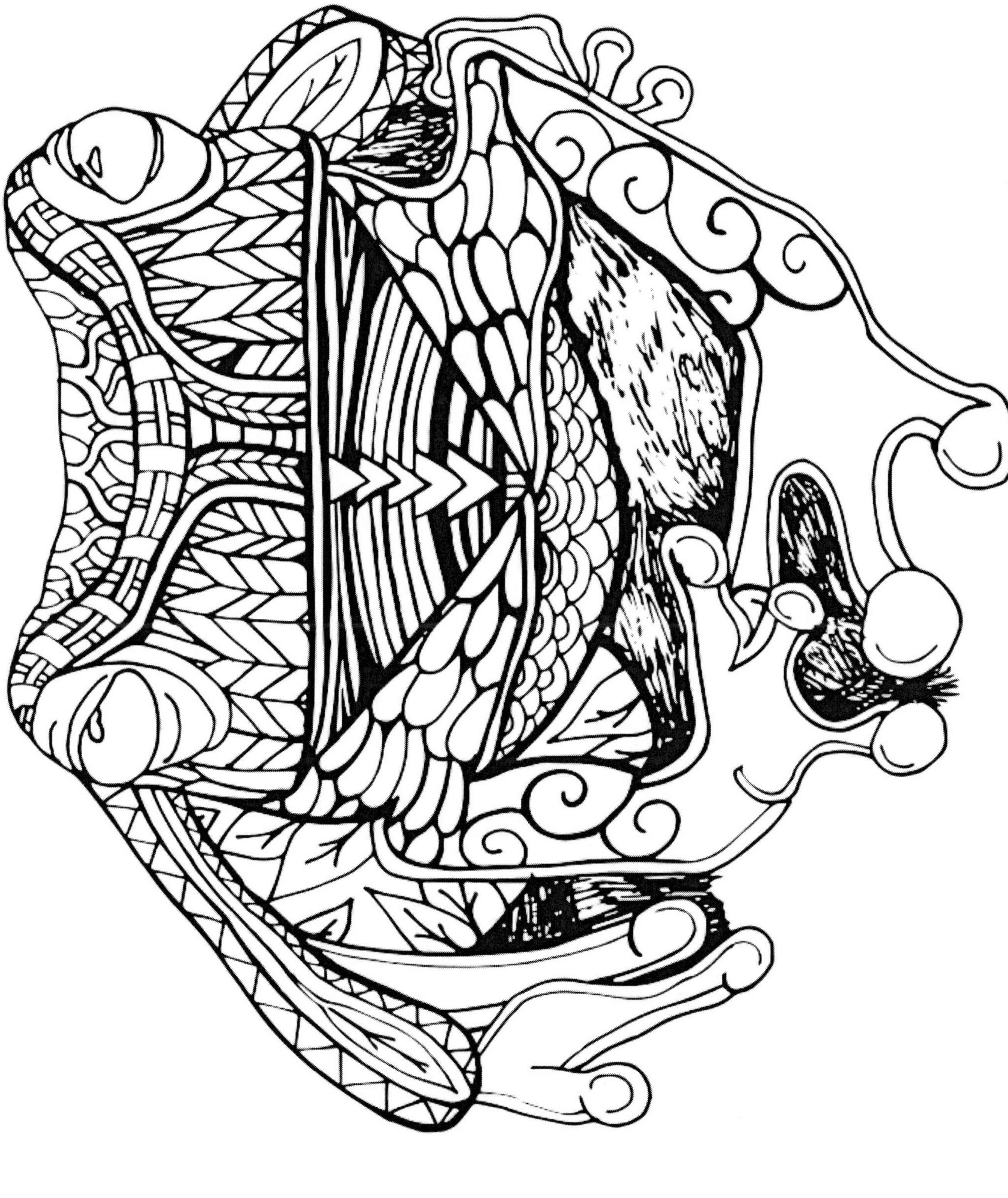

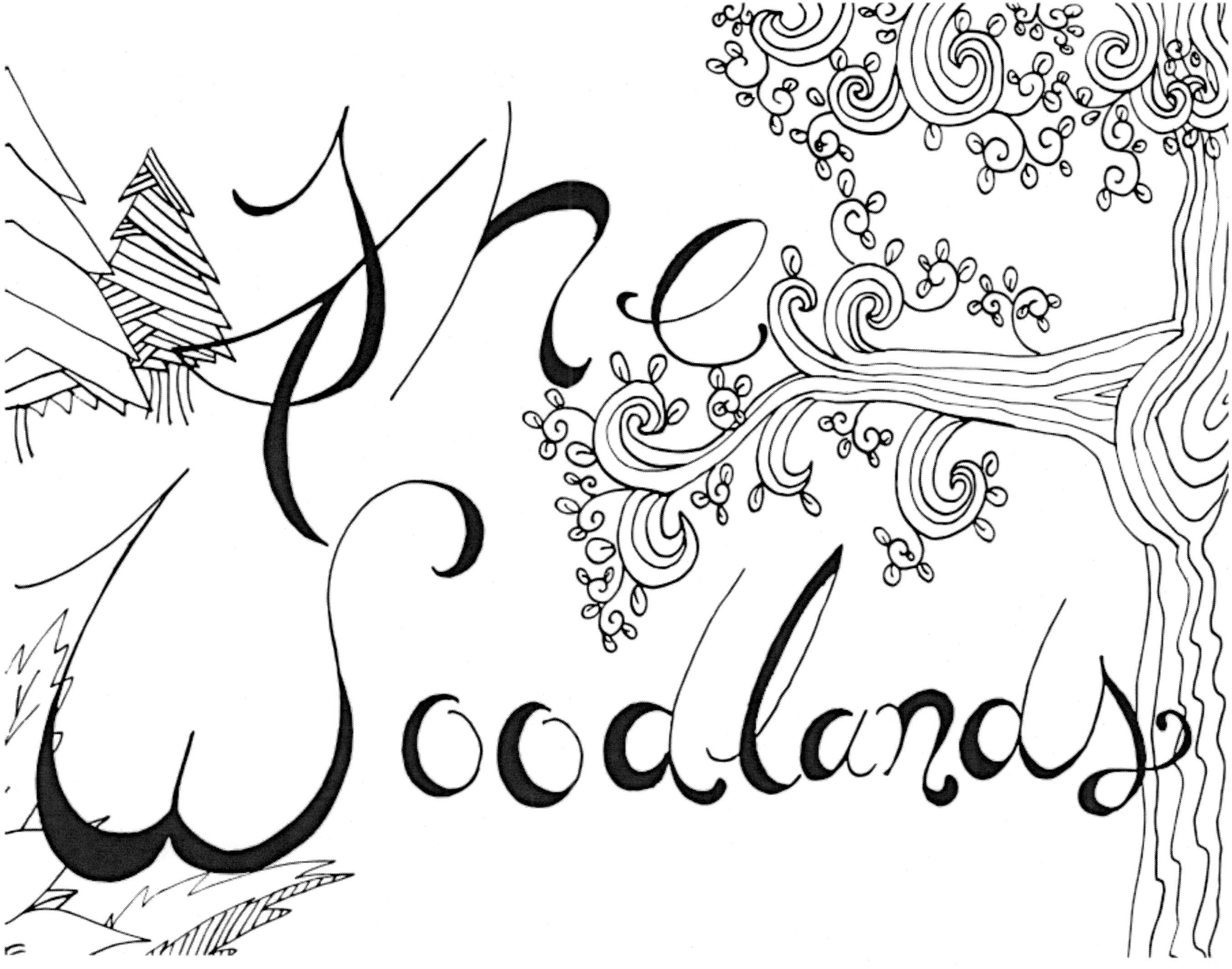
The Woodlands

Alpaca

- **Fun Facts**
  - Alpacas are gentle, curious creatures that spend most of their time in herds. They are so emotionally attached to each other that they become stressed out when separated from other alpacas that they share a bond with.
  - The oldest known record of alpacas dates back 1,000 before the great pyramids of Giza were ever built.
  - Inca nobles used to demonstrate their wealth by how many alpacas they owned.
  - Alpaca fleece has no lanolin, so it's hypoallergenic.
  - Alpacas don't bite. Not only do they not really have the strong dental capacity to pull it off, but they are unlikely to try, as they maintain a very calm, friendly demeanor.
  - There are two types of Alpacas: the Huacaya (which has dense water-resistant fleece) and the Suri (which has a very luxurious fiber that is often woven into fine fabrics).
- **What do they Eat?**
  - Alpacas eat hay and pasture grass.
- **Where They Hang Out**
  - Alpacas originally come from Peru, although now they can be found throughout South America, Ecuador, Chile, and Bolivia.
- **Helpful Organization**
  - World Wildlife

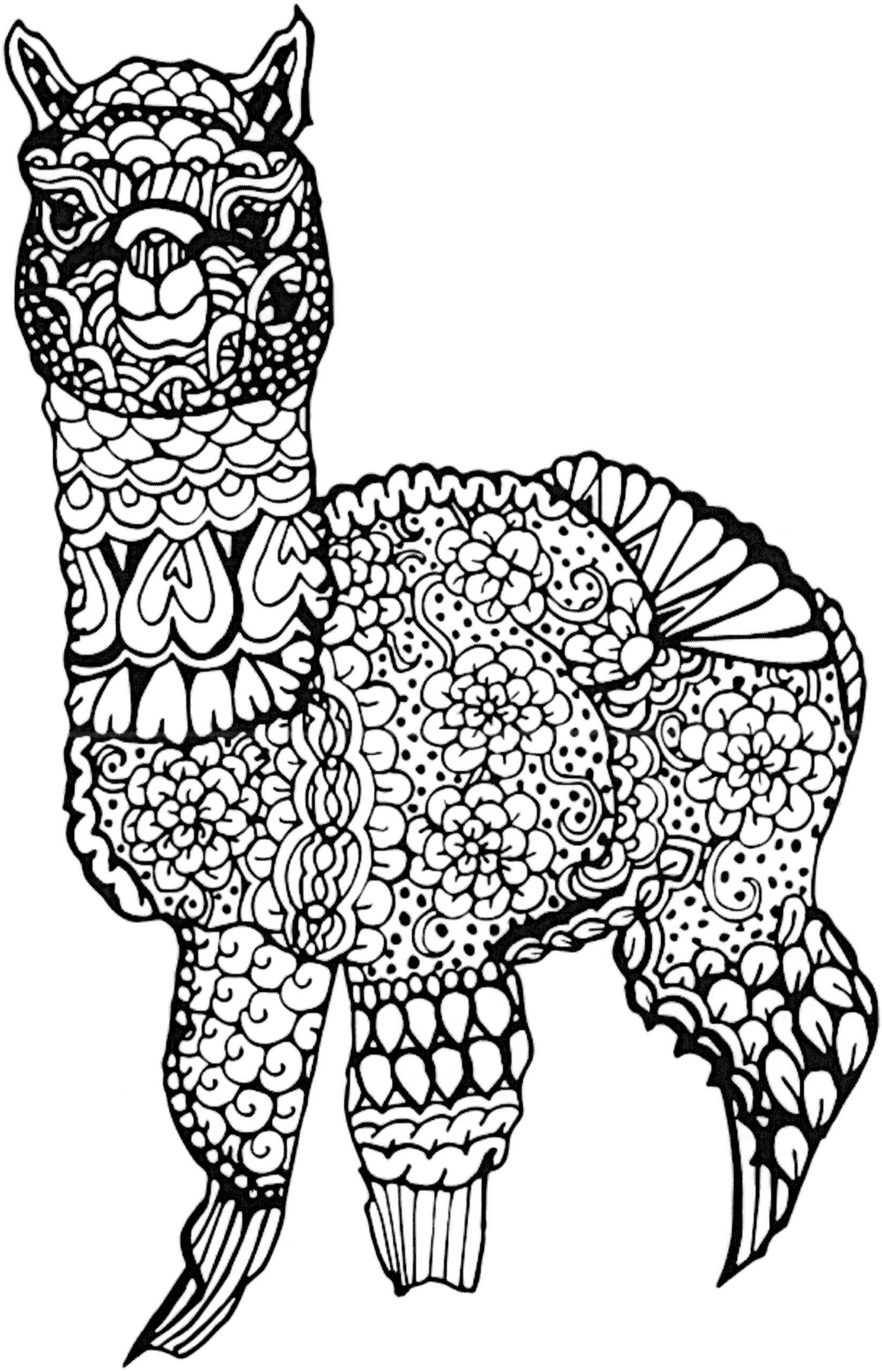

Cape Buffalo

- **Fun Facts**
  - Buffalo generally live up to 20 years in the wild.
  - Buffalo have poor senses. They can't really see or hear much of anything, but they can smell pretty well.
  - Buffalo feed at night, so they have a difficult time regulating their body temperature.
  - If a calf is in danger, they will bellow for help and herd members will find and attempt to help it.
  - Female buffalo will only have one calf every 1-2 years. They give birth during the rainy season.
  - Male buffaloes are solitary creatures, but females form large protective herds in which to raise their young.
  - Forest buffalo have shorter thorns than buffalo that spend their time out in open savannahs.
  - Buffalo have been known to ambush hunters in Africa.
- **What Do They Eat?**
  - Buffalo survive on grass.
- **Where They Hang Out**
  - Cape Buffalo live in dense forests and open plains throughout Africa. Regardless of their preference between the two habitats, they always try to stay as close to water as possible.
- **Helpful Organization**
  - African Wildlife Foundation

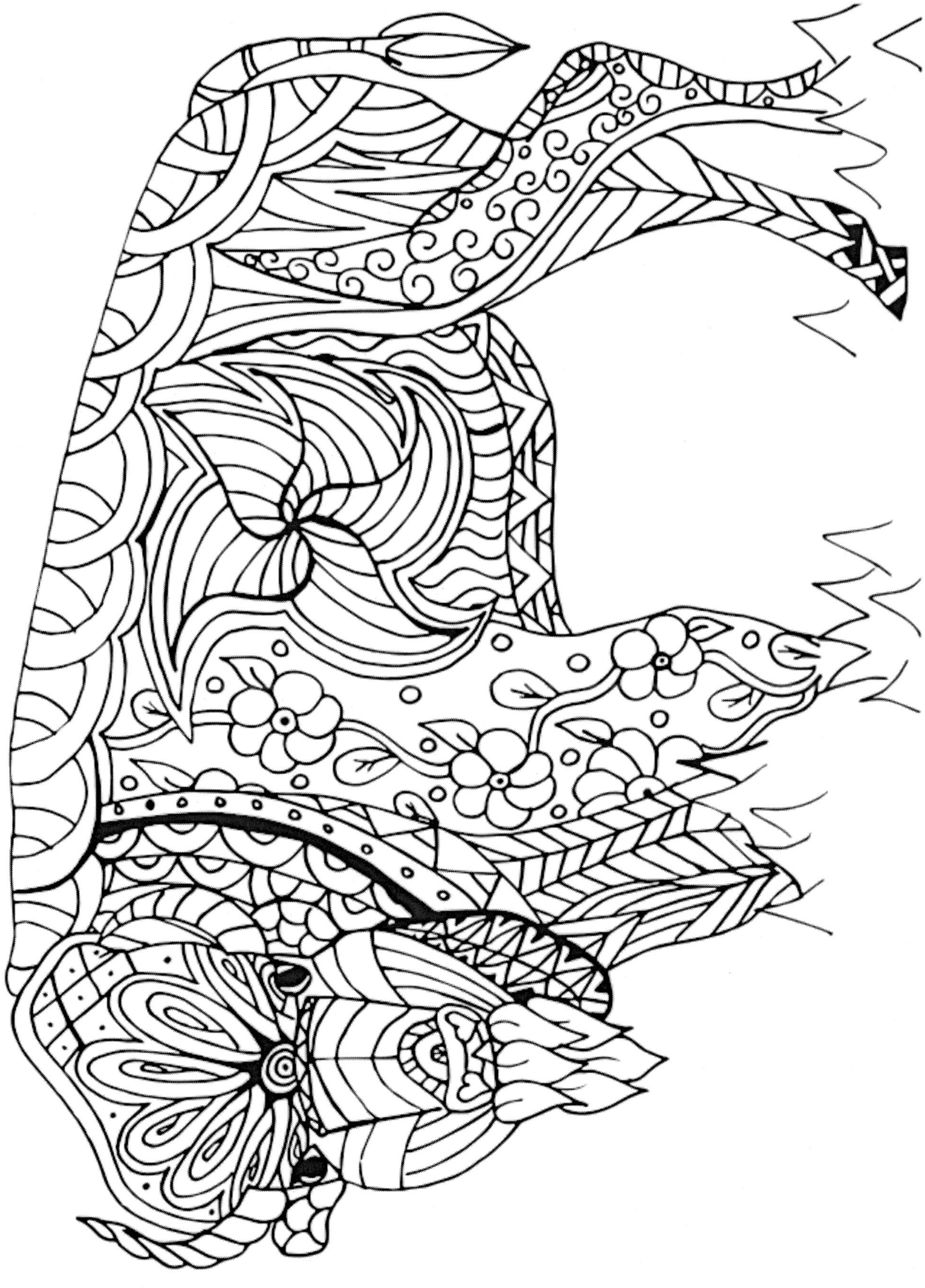

Cows

- **Fun Facts**
  - Mohammad Ghandi once described a cow as "a poem of compassion."
  - Cows have complex sleeping arrangements where their position is determined by their hierarchy in the herd.
  - Cows hold grudges for years and even show favoritism and ill-will toward one another, showing an advanced emotional development. When cows solve problems, they show signs of excitement and pride. Some even jump up in the air in triumph.
  - Cows produce the most milk when treated well and with respect. Their milk production increases even further when they are treated as individuals.
  - Cows are protected animals in Hinduism and are honored once a year on Gopastami, where they are washed and decorated in temples.
- **What Do They Eat?**
  - Cows graze on grass. They regurgitate their food and then chew it as cud to aid in digestion.
- **Where They Hang Out**
  - Cows can be found all over Europe, North America, and throughout India. They prefer grasslands.
- **Helpful Organization**
  - Mercy for Animals

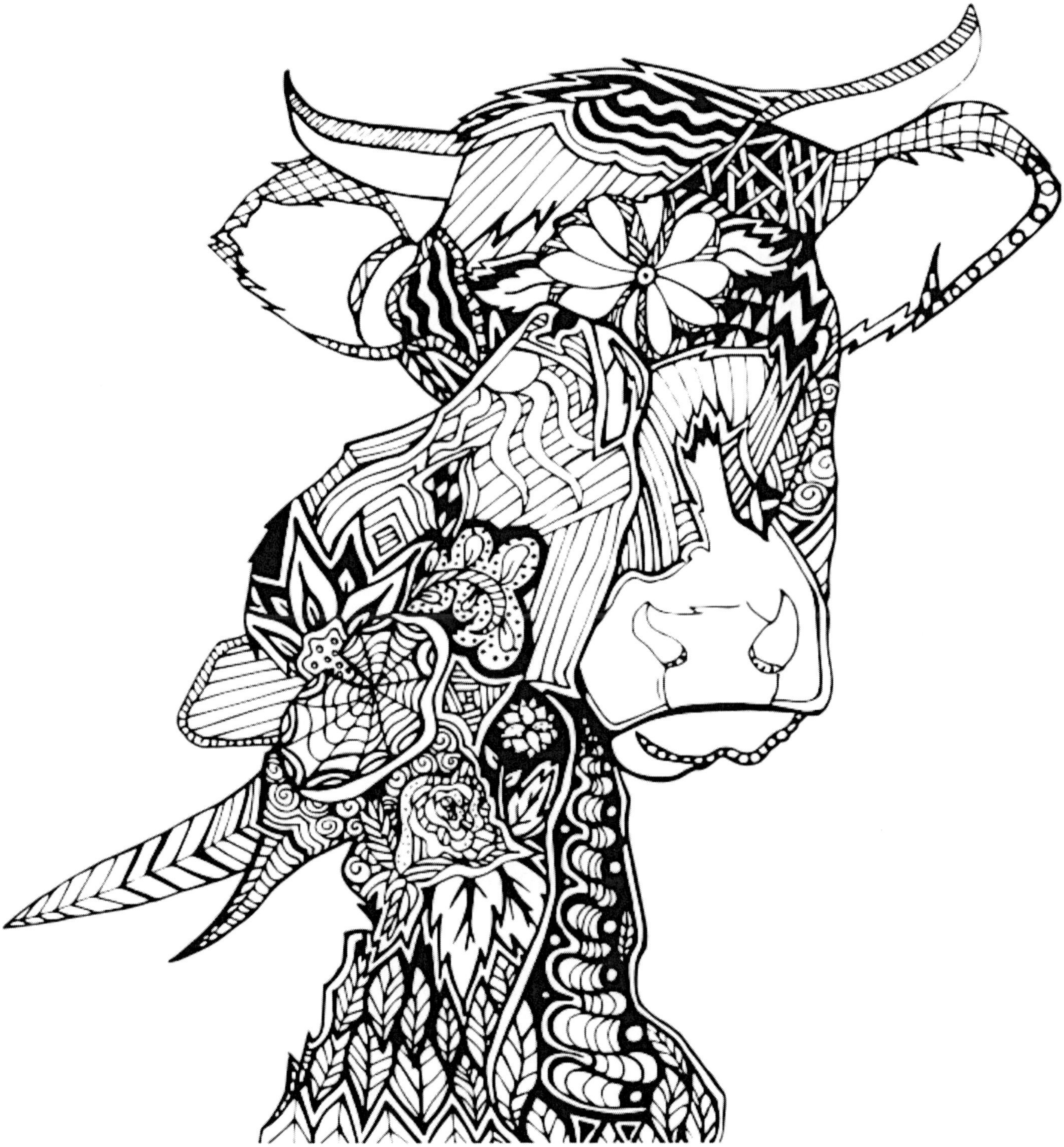

Grizzly Bears

- **Fun Facts**
  - Grizzly Bears have an advanced sense of smell that trumps even that of a hound dog.
  - Grizzlies range in color from light cream to dark brown and even black.
  - Grizzly bears tend to live fairly solitary lives. They are not overly territorial unless a mother fears that her cubs are in danger, in which case she will become positively volatile.
  - A Grizzly bear mother will stay with her cubs and raise them for up to 3 years before letting them go out on their own. Not only do grizzly bear fathers not participate in raising their young, but they can also pose a threat. For that reason, grizzly couples stay away from one another during parenting.
  - Grizzlies will significantly increase their caloric intake during the later part of the summer so that they will put on weight in preparation for their winter hibernation.
- **What Do They Eat?**
  - Grizzly bears have a fairly diverse diet. They are omnivores and will eat seeds, roots, berries, fish, elk, deer, and insects. They have also been known to graze on grass.
- **Where They Hang Out**
  - Grizzly bears favor the denser forests of North America.
- **Helpful Organization**
  - Defenders of Wildlife

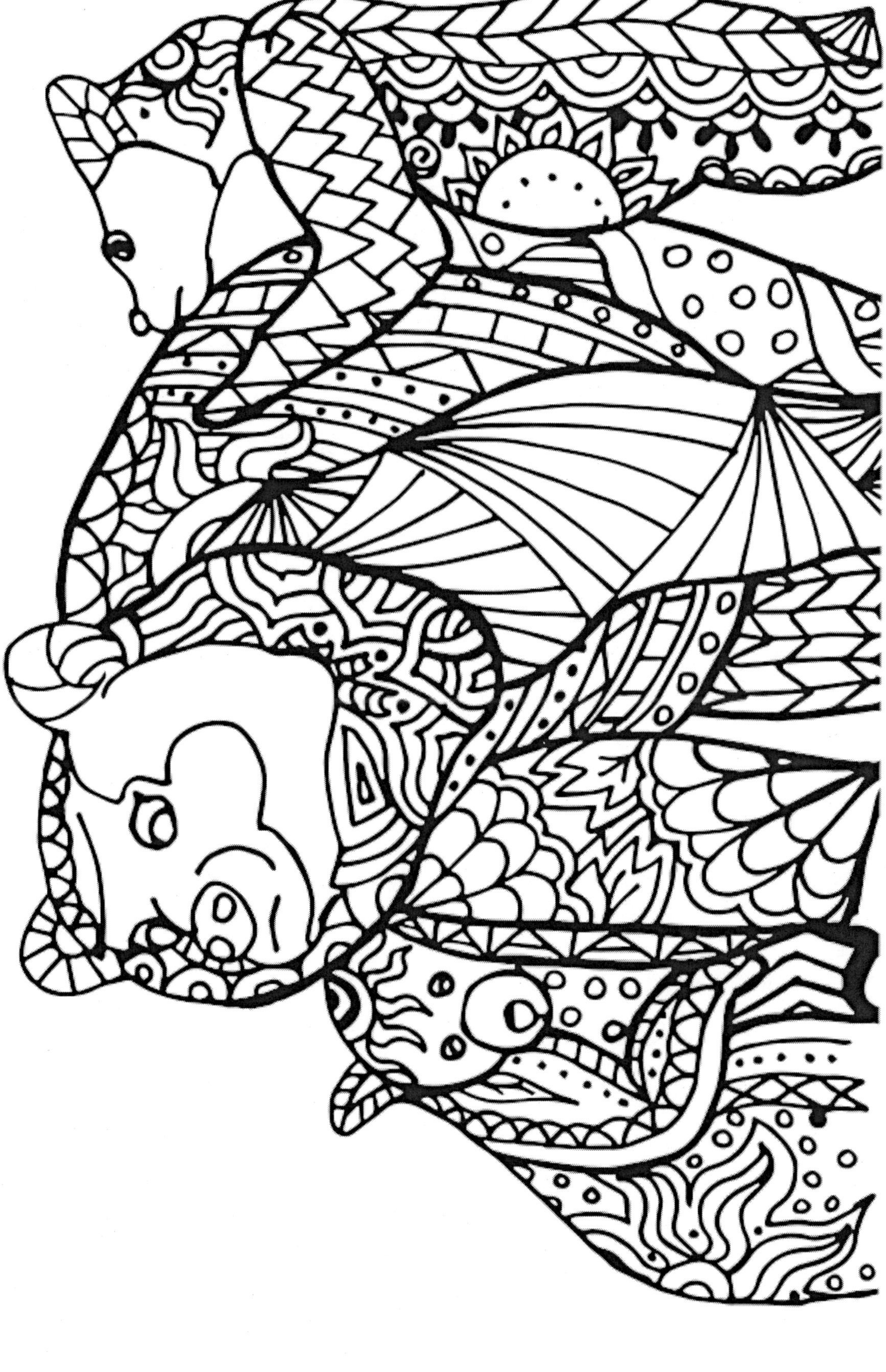

Deer

- **Fun Facts**
  - The world's largest deer went extinct 11,000 years ago. It was up to 7 feet from hooves to shoulder and had massive antlers that reached 12 feet.
  - Deer have distinctive antlers that grow up from boney supporting structures.
  - There are some breeds of deer that are monogamous creatures.
  - Deer babies are called *calves*.
  - Deer range from dark brown to a light cream color. Fawns are born with white spots that aid in camouflaging.
  - There are 47 different species of deer.
  - The Chinese Water Deer doesn't have antlers. Instead, it has large canine teeth.
- **What Do They Eat?**
  - Deer eat grass, leaves, and small shrubs. Deer chew their cud to fully digest their food.
- **Where They Hang Out**
  - Deer live in rainforests, grasslands, mountains, wetlands and in forests all over the world. The only two places they don't inhabit are Antarctica and Australia.
- **Helpful Organization**
  - National Wildlife Federation

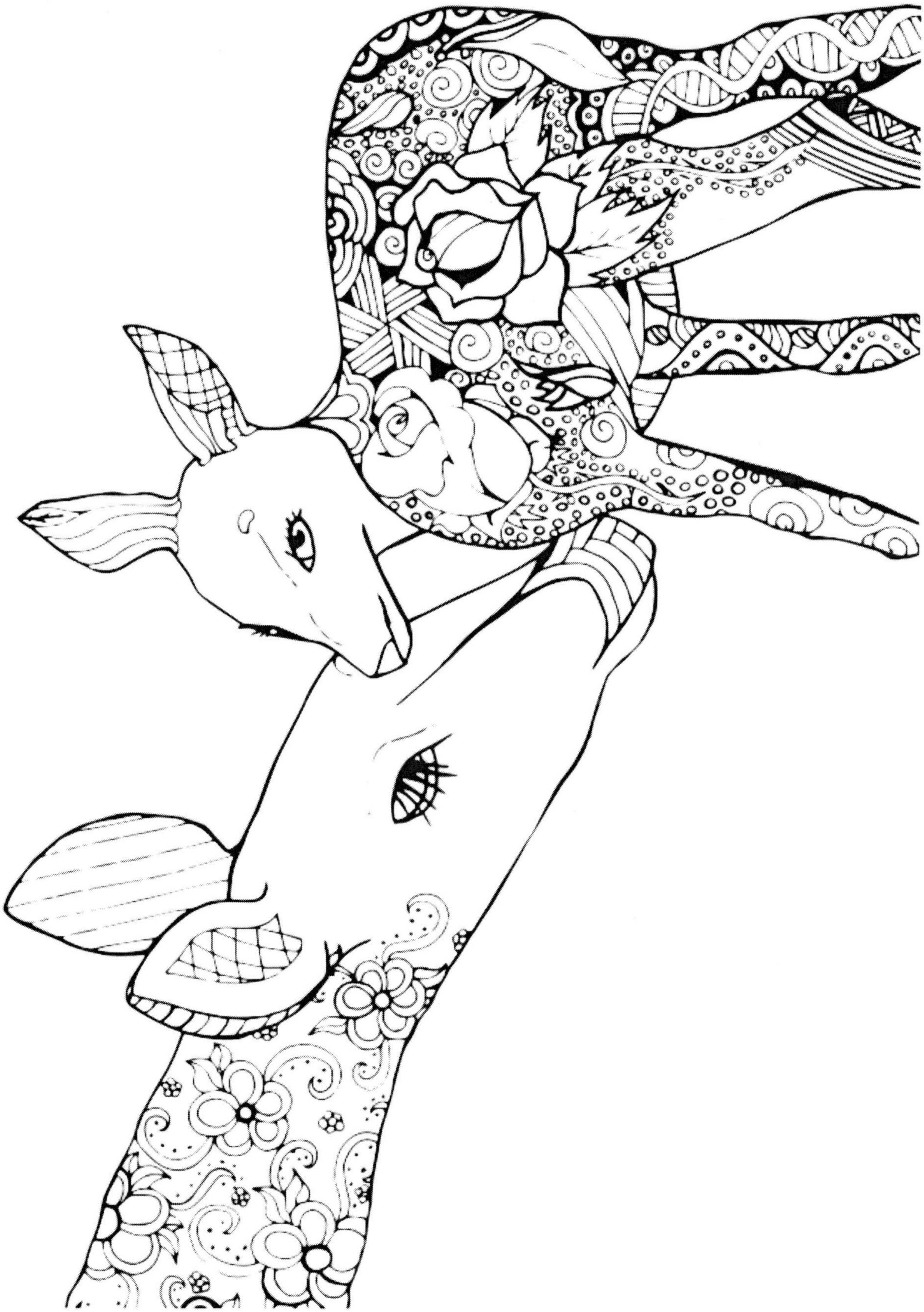

Goat

- **Fun Facts**
    - Goats can jump up to 5 feet in the air.
    - Goats do not have tear ducts.
    - There are over 120 million goats in China alone.
    - When Abraham Lincoln was in office, his sons had two pet goats that lived at the white house with them.
    - Male goats are called *bucks,* female goats are called *does,* and young goats are referred to as *kids.*
    - When a doe gives birth to a healthy kid, the young goat can stand within an hour and is immediately able to keep up with its herd.
    - Does typically produce between 1 and 3 litters every two years.
    - A human can digest goat's milk within 20 minutes. It would take that same person a full day to digest cow's milk.
- **What Do They Eat?**
    - Goats are herbivores that spend most of their days eating clover and grass.
- **Where They Hang Out**
    - Goats originally came from the Mid-East and Asia. Now, they can be found in North America, too.
- **Helpful Organization**
    - Rare Breed Goats Co.

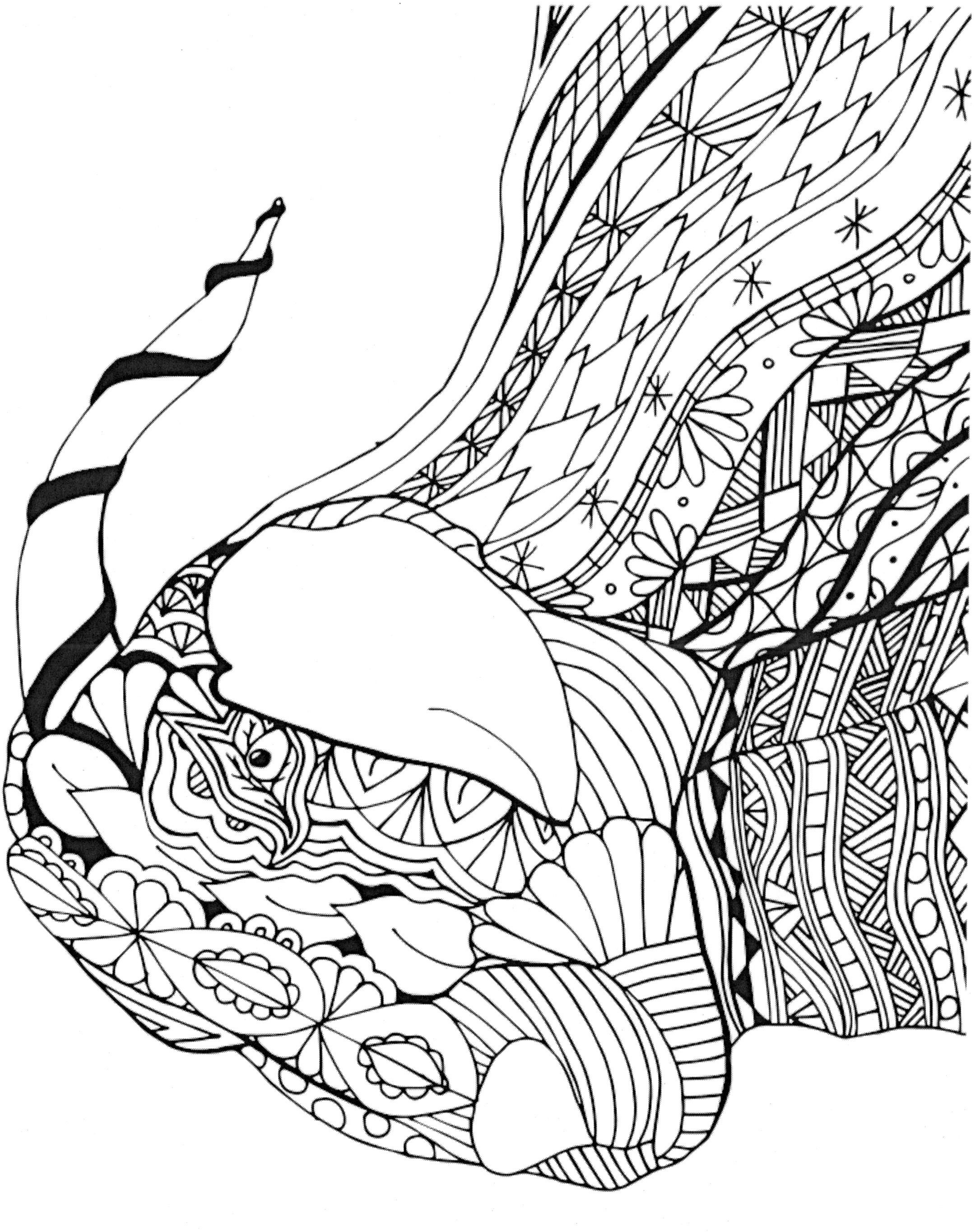

Fox

- **Fun Facts**
  - Foxes are, on average, just slightly bigger than domestic house cats.
  - Male foxes are called *dogs,* while female foxes are referred to as *vixen*. Baby foxes are called *cubs*.
  - Foxes can live up to 14 years in the wild.
  - While foxes do go out during the day, they prefer to be nocturnal creatures.
  - Foxes use a fairly advanced language system comprised of up to 28 different calls to communicate with one another.
  - Foxes run up to 30 mph.
  - While they are technically distant cousins to wolves, foxes actually have the most in common with cats, both physically and behaviorally.
- **What Do They Eat?**
  - Foxes eat a variety of different things, from worms and spiders, to berries. They actually act like guided missiles, harnessing the earth's magnetic field to hunt their prey.
- **Where They Hang Out**
  - Red foxes live in North America and Europe. There is also a white breed that lives in the Arctic.
- **Helpful Organization**
  - The Fox Project

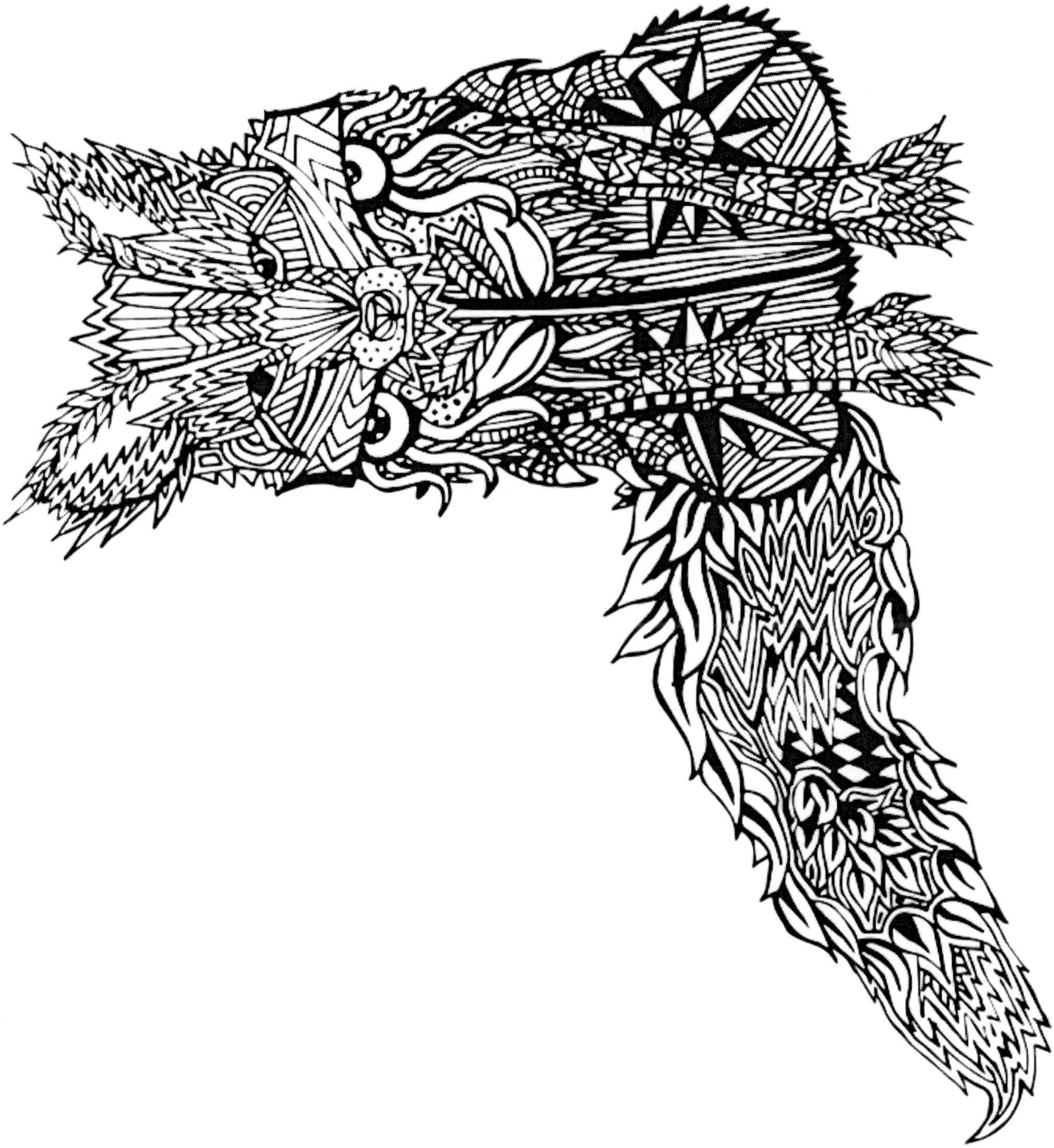

Boar

- **Fun Facts**
  - Wild boars can grow up to 6-1/2 feet in length, 40 inches high, and can weigh anywhere between 100 and 700 pounds. They can live up to 10 years in the wild.
  - Wild boars have a double coat of fur that can be either brown, black, red or gray.
  - Wild boars use their rubbery snouts to dig up underground roots and bulbs.
  - A mother wild boar will give birth to 2-6 piglets. When they are born, young boar are covered in cream-colored stripes that help them camouflage with the landscape.
  - Wild boar are nocturnal, spending most of their time at night foraging for food. During the day, they sleep in dense nests made of leaves.
  - Wild boar may have poor eyesight but their sense of smell is incredible.
- **What do they Eat?**
  - Wild boars are omnivorous creatures. They eat mice, eggs, berries, lizards, worms, fruits, leaves, and snakes.
- **Where They Hang Out**
  - Wild boars live in Africa, Asia, and Europe.
- **Helpful Organization**
  - The Wild Boar Conservation Association

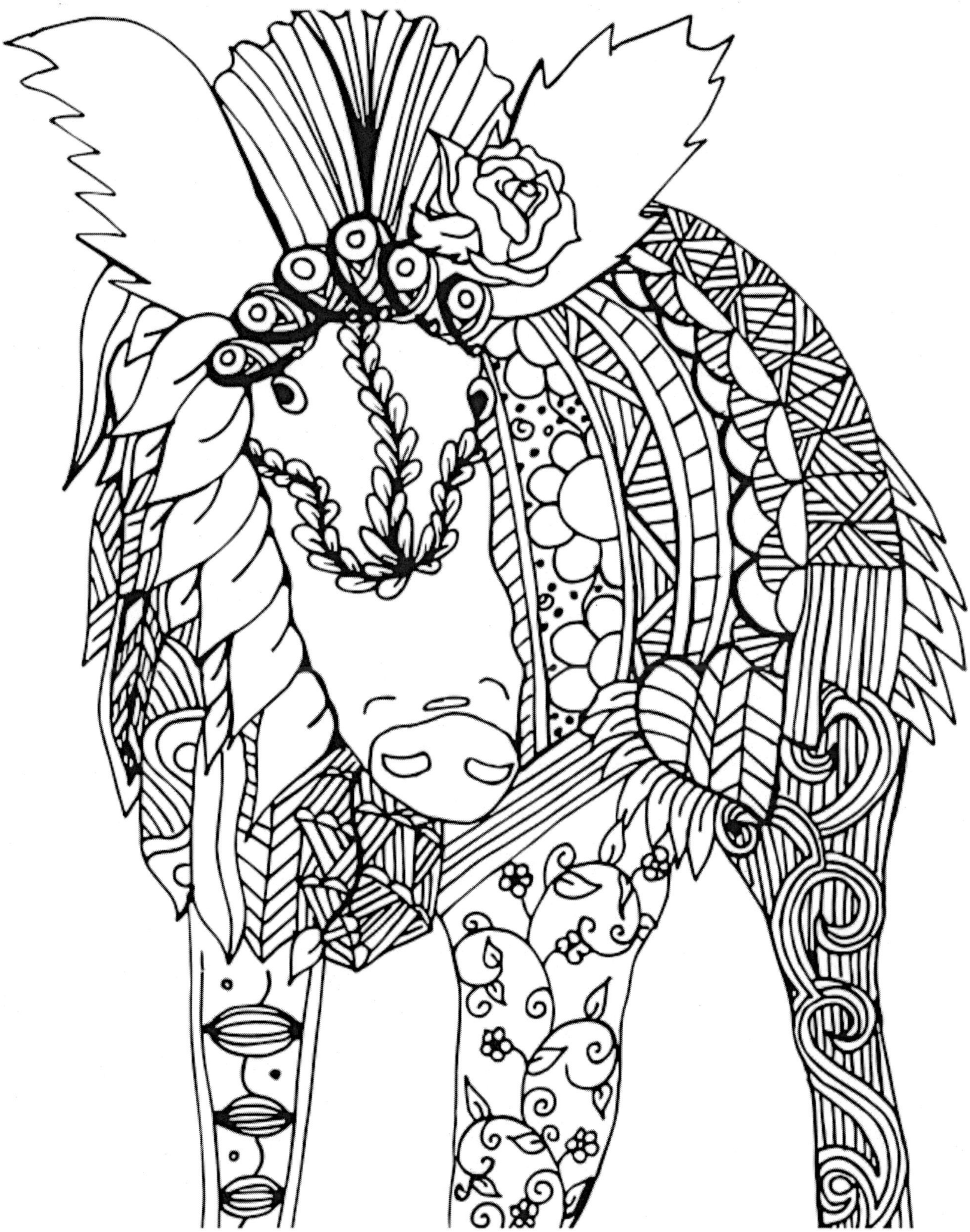

Wolf

- **Fun Facts**
  - Wolves can be gray, black or white. They have 42 teeth and weigh only 1 pound at birth. Female wolves can grow up to be almost 80 lbs, and males can top out at nearly 110 lbs.
  - A wolf litter ranges between 4 to 6 pups.
  - Wolves can live up to 13 years in the wild, although they average between 6 and 8 years.
  - Wolves can sprint between 36 and 38 mph.
  - The average wolf pack consists of 5 to 8 wolves, although some are as small as two individuals and others are as large as 40 wolves in total.
  - Wolves are monogamous creatures until one member of the couple dies.
  - Wolves have two layers of fur: an undercoat and an overcoat. This helps them withstand frigid temperature drops. During the spring and summer, they generally shed part of their coat to keep cooler.
- **What Do They Eat?**
  - Wolves prefer to feast on hoofed animals like caribou, deer, moose, bison, and elk.
- **Where They Hang Out**
  - Wolves can be found throughout North America, the Arctic, Europe, Asia, and North Africa.
- **Helpful Organization**
  - Wolf Haven International

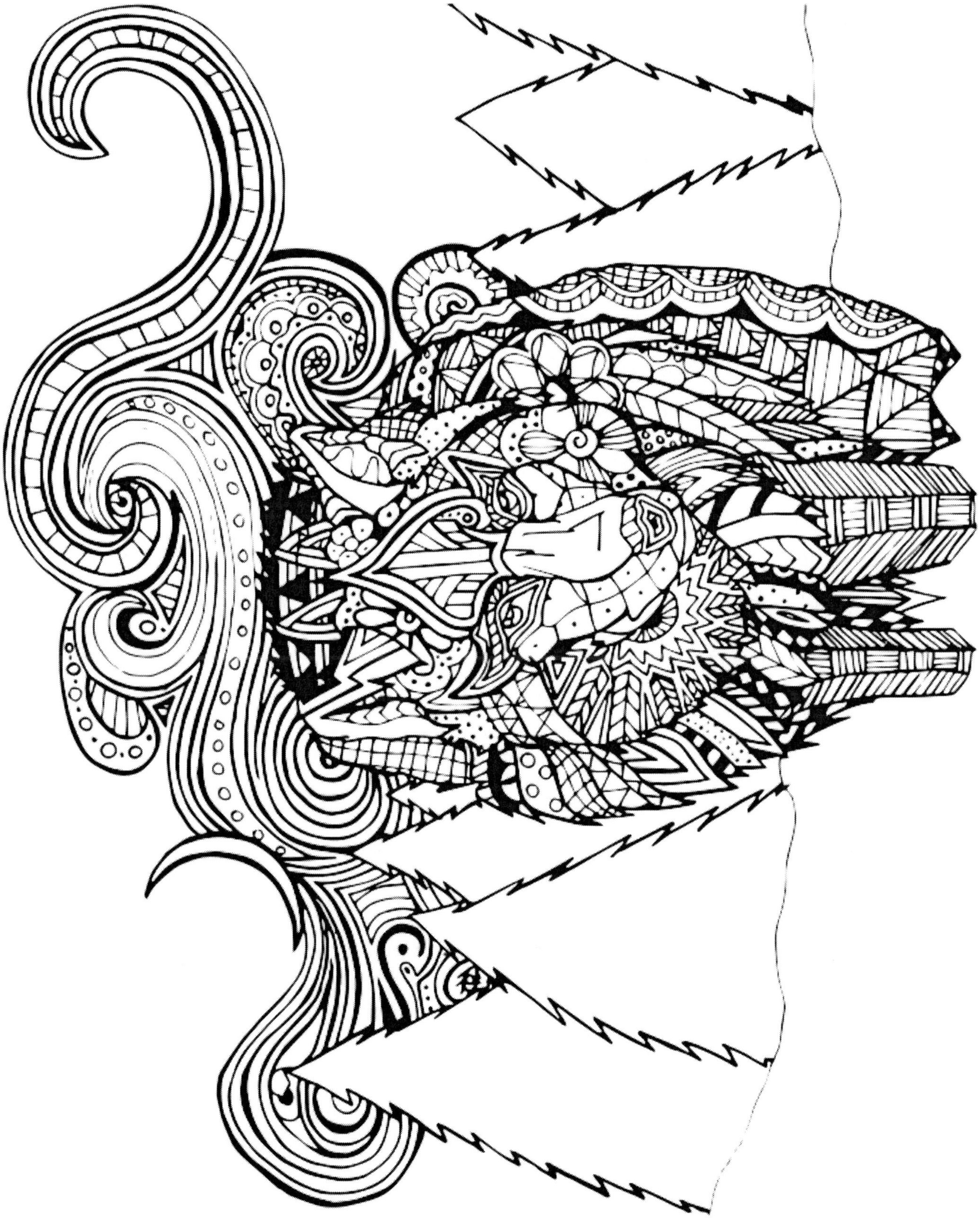

Texas Longhorn

- **Fun Facts**
  - There are actually two unrelated breeds of Longhorns: Texas (or American) Longhorns, and English Longhorns.
  - A longhorn's horns can extend 120 inches from tip-to-tip.
  - Longhorns actually come in a variety of different colors including some rare hues of lavender and mulberry.
  - Longhorns are able to go long distances and periods of time without water.
  - Longhorn calves are able to stand up sooner than any other breed of cattle.
  - Texas longhorns can breed well into their teens. There have been some that have managed to continue breeding for up to thirty years, making them highly desirable among breeders.
- **What do they Eat?**
  - Longhorns graze on a large range of vegetation (unlike traditional cows and other cattle, which survive mostly on grass). They will eat bushes, flowers, wild roses , lilacs, grass, etc. They'll even eat the thorns in rose bushes.
- **Where They Hang Out**
  - Texas Longhorns live exclusively in North America, as they are the result of cross-breeding between Spanish wild stock and domestic cattle.
- **Helpful Organization**
  - Longhorn HERD

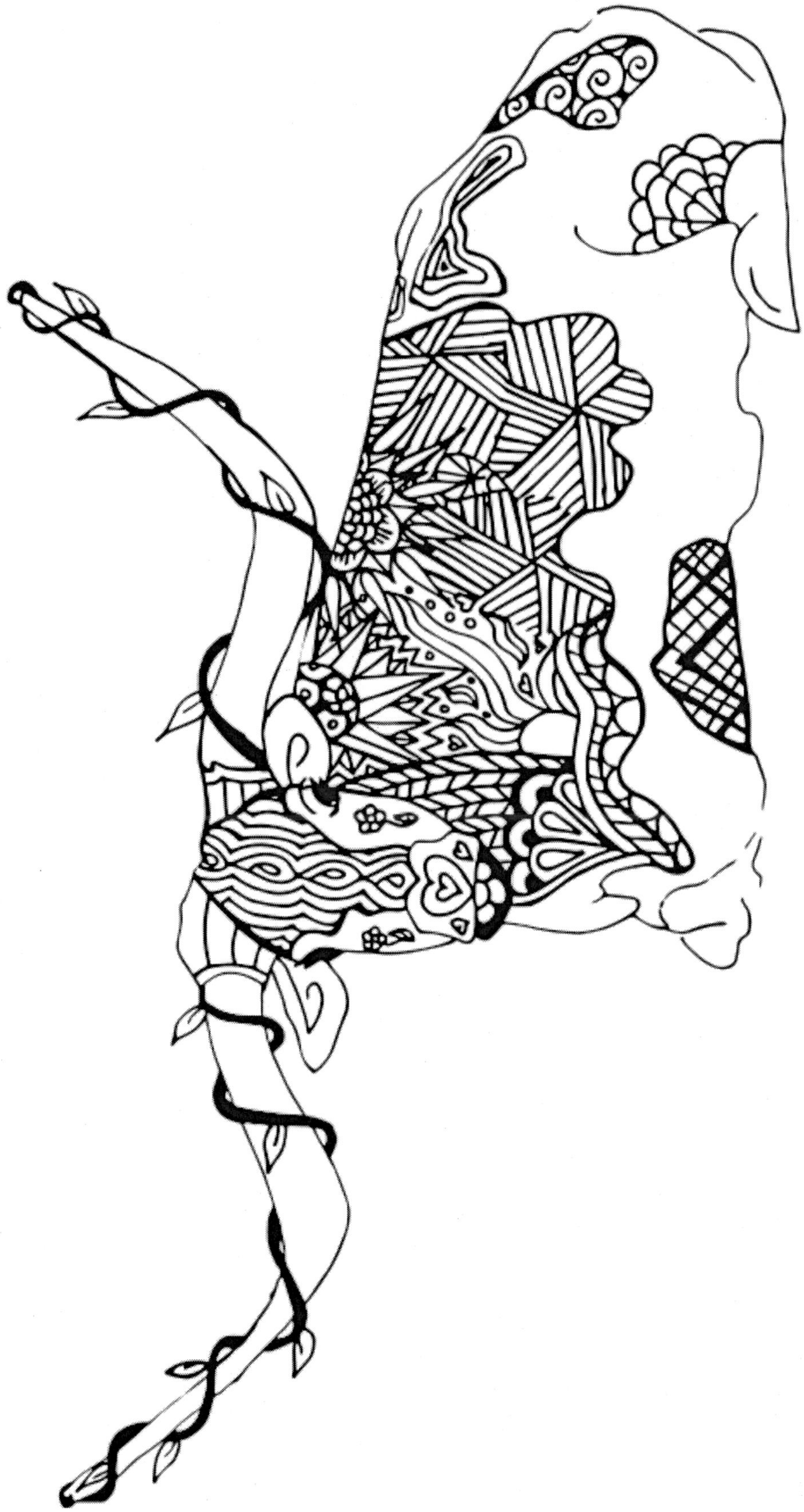

Lamb

- **Fun Facts**
    - Sheep have advanced emotions and are able to display them physically. One indicator of their mood is the positioning and movement of their ears.
    - Sheep are able to remember and recognize up to 50 individual sheep and humans. Sheep are even able to form bonds with certain members of their herd and are known for having best friends.
    - Egyptians thought that sheep were sacred. When sheep died, they were often mummified.
    - In the Chinese zodiac, sheep represent righteousness, compassion, gentleness and sincerity.
    - Male sheep are called rams, female sheep are called *ewes,* and baby sheep are called *lambs.*
    - When sheep fall over, they are unable to right themselves. If there is nobody to help them back up, they will stay that way and likely die within the day.
    - When Woodrow Wilson was in office, his wife had sheep graze on the white house lawn to keep it trimmed.
- **What Do They Eat?**
    - Sheep graze on grasses, weeds, grains, and clover.
- **Where They Hang Out**
    - Sheep live throughout North America, Asia, and Europe.
- **Helpful Organizations**
    - Wild Sheep Foundation

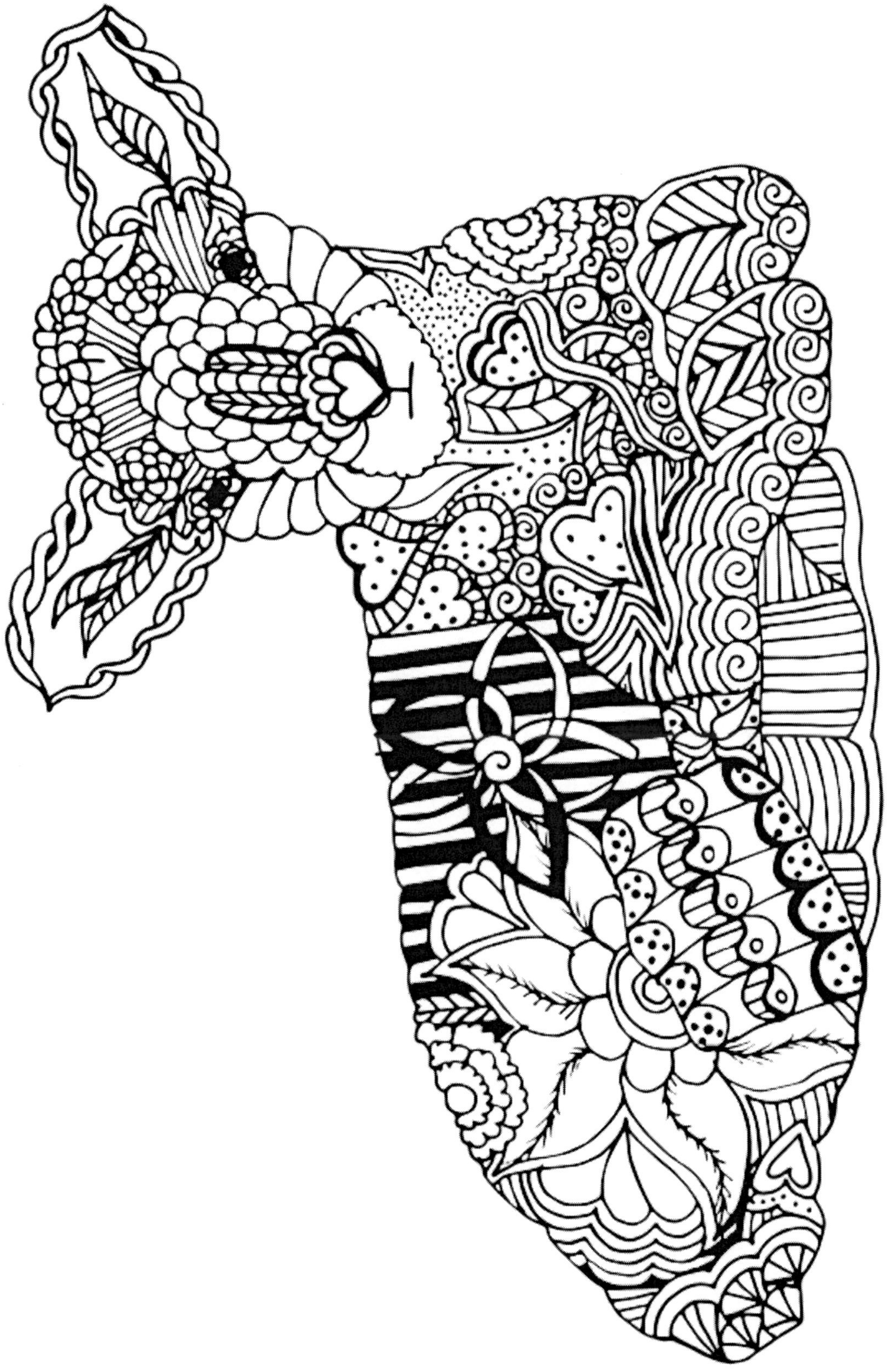

Hare

- **Fun Facts**
    - There are two main types of wild hares: Arctic and Brown.
    - A hare's coat will change with the season. In the summer, it's a blue-gray color and then, in the winter, it changes to an almost pure white. This helps it camouflage with its surroundings year-round.
    - Hares can be either social or solitary creatures and can live up to 12 years in the wild.
    - Arctic hares give birth to a single litter of up to 8 *leverets* per year. Brown hares will give birth to up to 3 litters of up to per year. Unlike their rabbit cousins, (who give birth in nests), hares give birth on the ground.
    - Hares can sprint up to 35 mph.
    - Female hares are called *does,* while male hares are called *bucks.* A group of hares is either a *down* or a *warren.*
    - When hares are trying to hide, they keep close to the ground and hold their ears flat against their backs.
- **What Do They Eat?**
    - Hares are herbivores that survive on berries, crops, roots, and broad-leaved plants.
- **Where They Hang Out**
    - Hares live in nests above the ground all over the world. They do not burrow the way rabbits do.
- **Helpful Organization**
    - Hare Conservation Trust

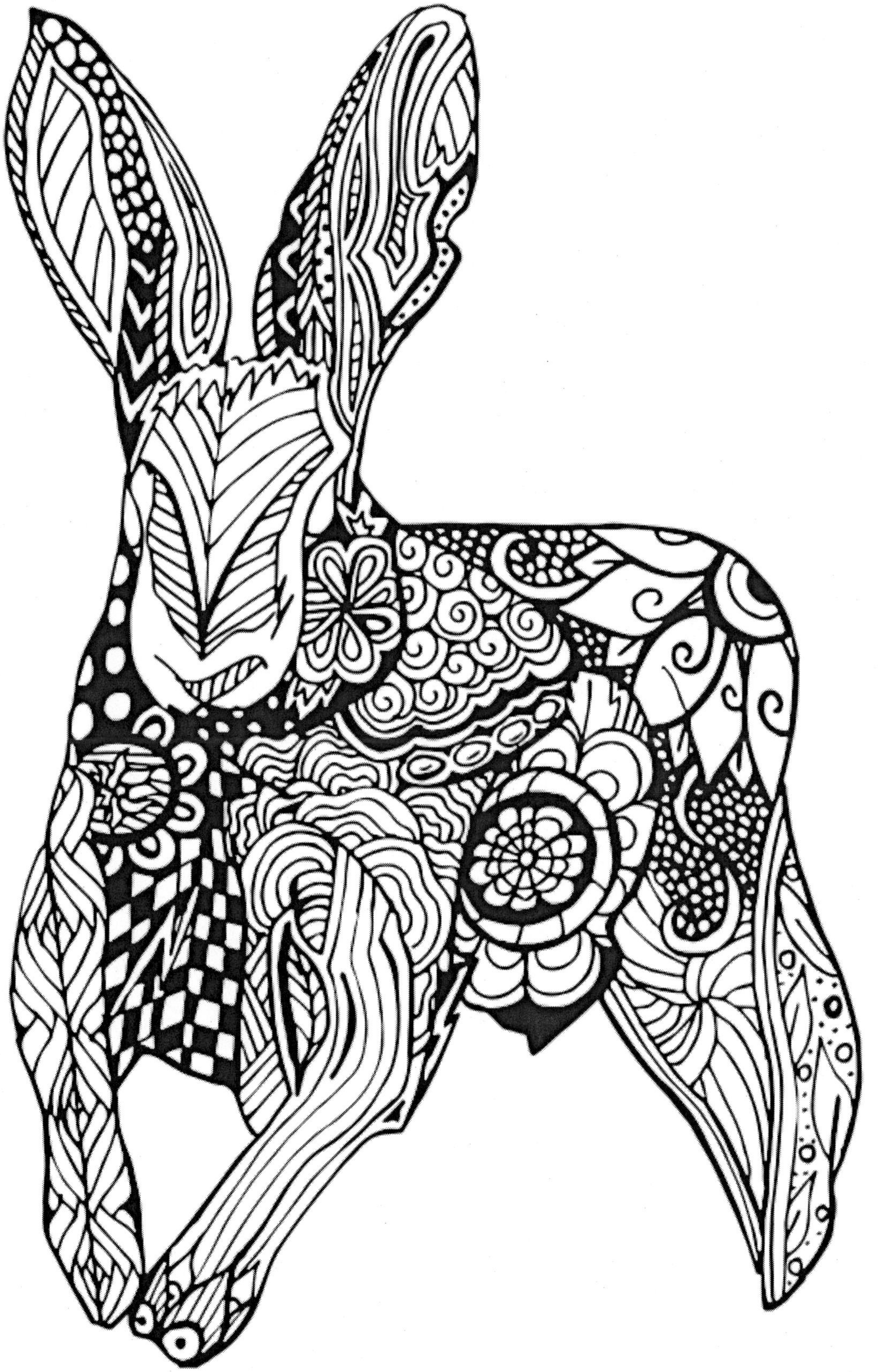

Horse

- **Fun Facts**
  - Horses have been around for more than 50 million years, but they were first domesticated in Asia between 3,000 and 4,000 B.C.E.
  - Horse range in size, weighing as little as 120 lbs and as much as 2,200 lbs.
  - Horses use their ears, eyes, and nostrils to express their moods.
  - Horses have nearly 360-degree vision. Their blind spots are directly behind them and directly in front of them.
  - Horses communicate with one another using a series of different vocalizations.
  - Horses are highly intelligent creatures. They have shown signs of understanding concept formation and categorization techniques.
  - Horses have a higher sense of smell and hearing than humans.
- **What Do They Eat?**
  - Each one of the some 400 breeds of horses is herbivorous. They eat grass, oats, barely, and hay.
- **Where They Hang Out**
  - Horses can be found everywhere on Earth, with the exception of Antarctica.
- **Helpful Organization**
  - Return to Freedom

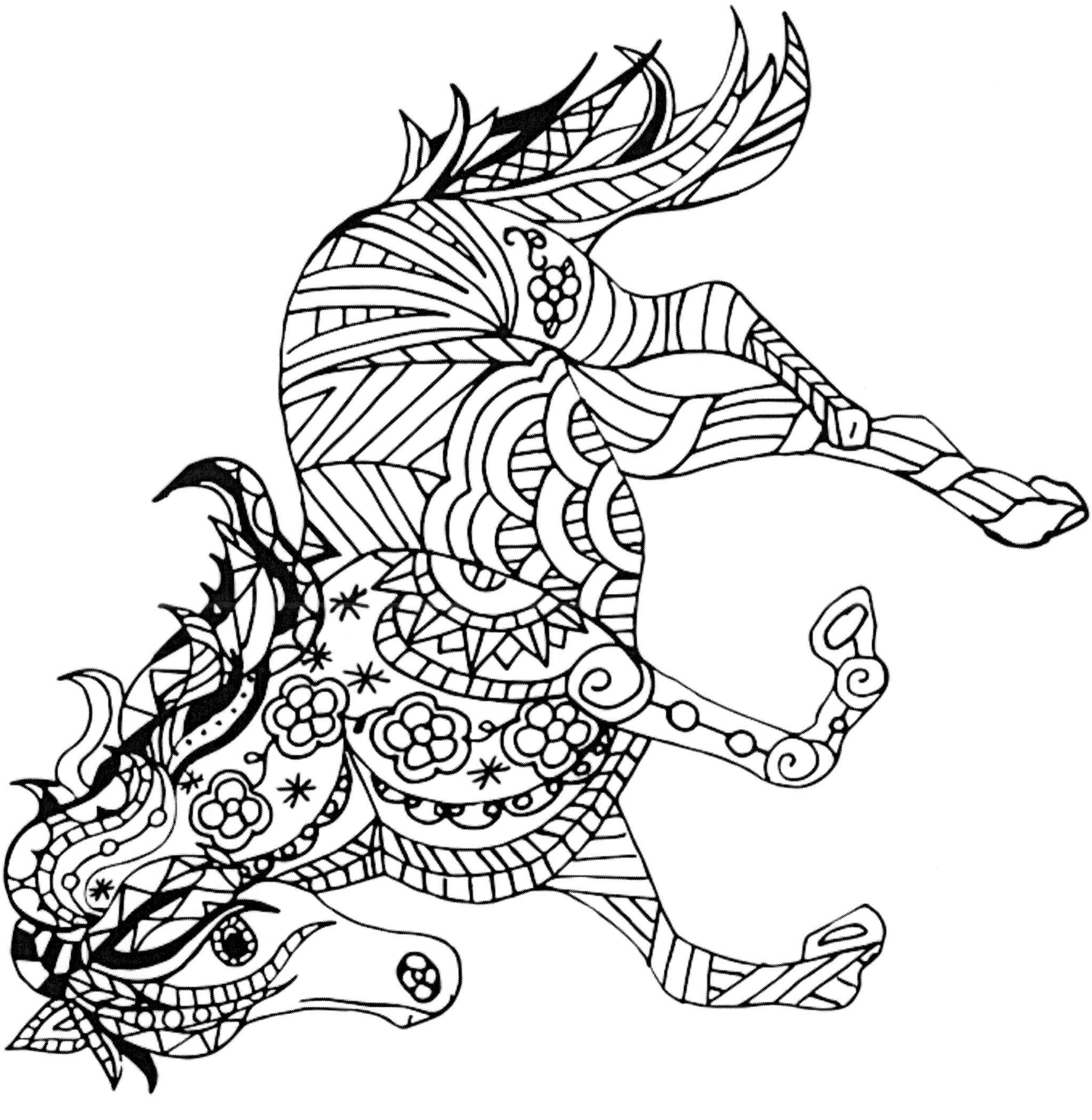

Moose

- **Fun Facts**
  - Moose can sprint up to 35 mph and can maintain a steady pace of 20 mph over longer distances.
  - Female moose give birth to 1-2 calves at a time. Those calves will stay with their mother for a year.
  - Moose are good swimmers and will paddle for miles. Sometimes, they even submerge themselves underwater.
  - Moose antlers can span up to 6 feet from end-to-end.
  - Moose are most active at sunset and sunrise.
  - Moose are similar to cows in that they have 4 chambers in their stomachs. Because of this, they chew their food, regurgitate it, and then chew the cud to aid in digestion.
  - In the wild, moose can live between 15 and 20 years.
- **What Do They Eat?**
  - In the summertime, moose will graze on grasses and shrubs. In the winter, they survive on shrubs, mosses, and pine-cones. They will eat aquatic plants at and below the surface of melting lakes in the spring.
- **Where They Hang Out**
  - Moose can be found in Asia, Europe, and North America. They tend to stay in areas where it snows.
- **Helpful Organization**
  - Alaska Moose Conservation Fund

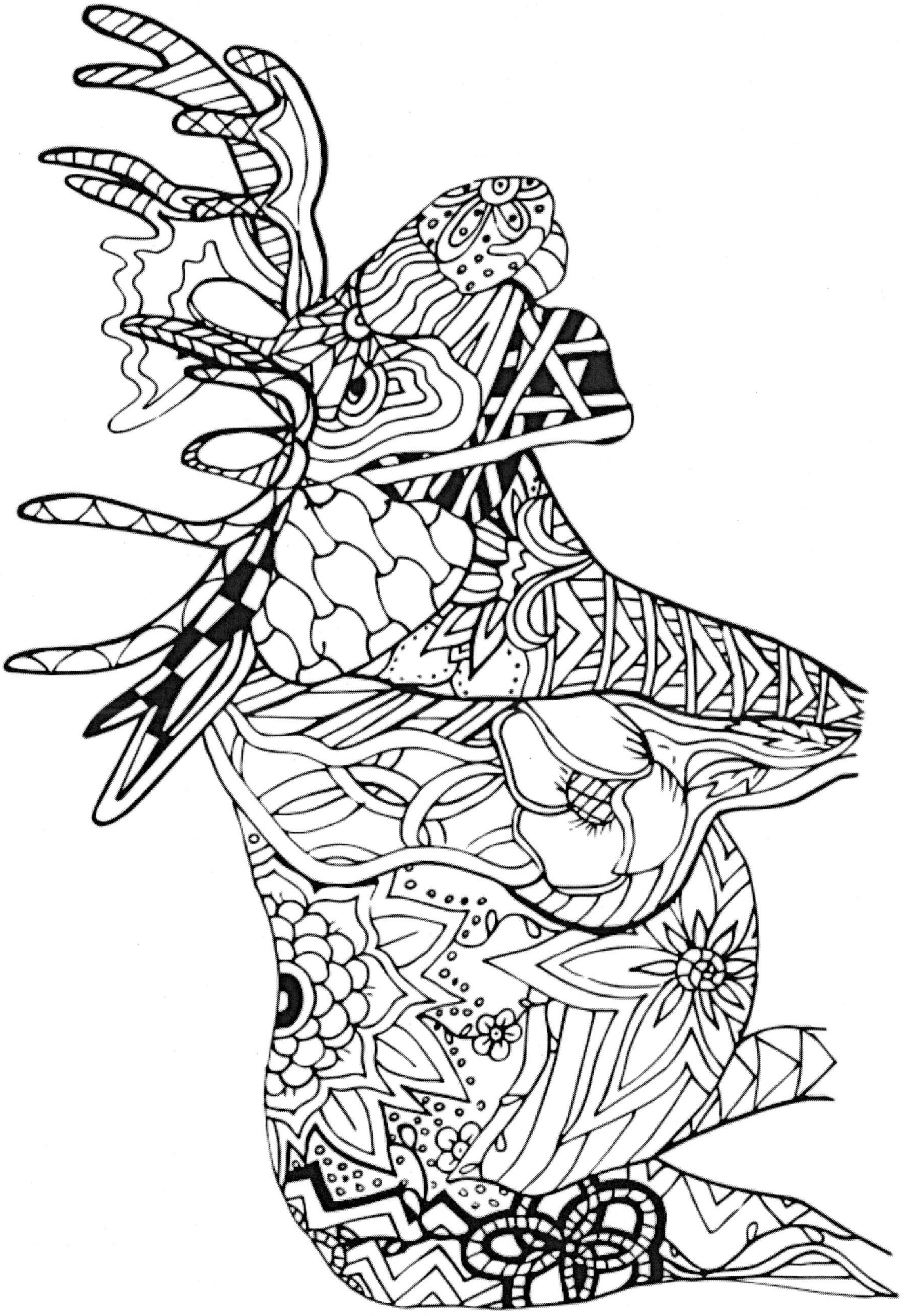

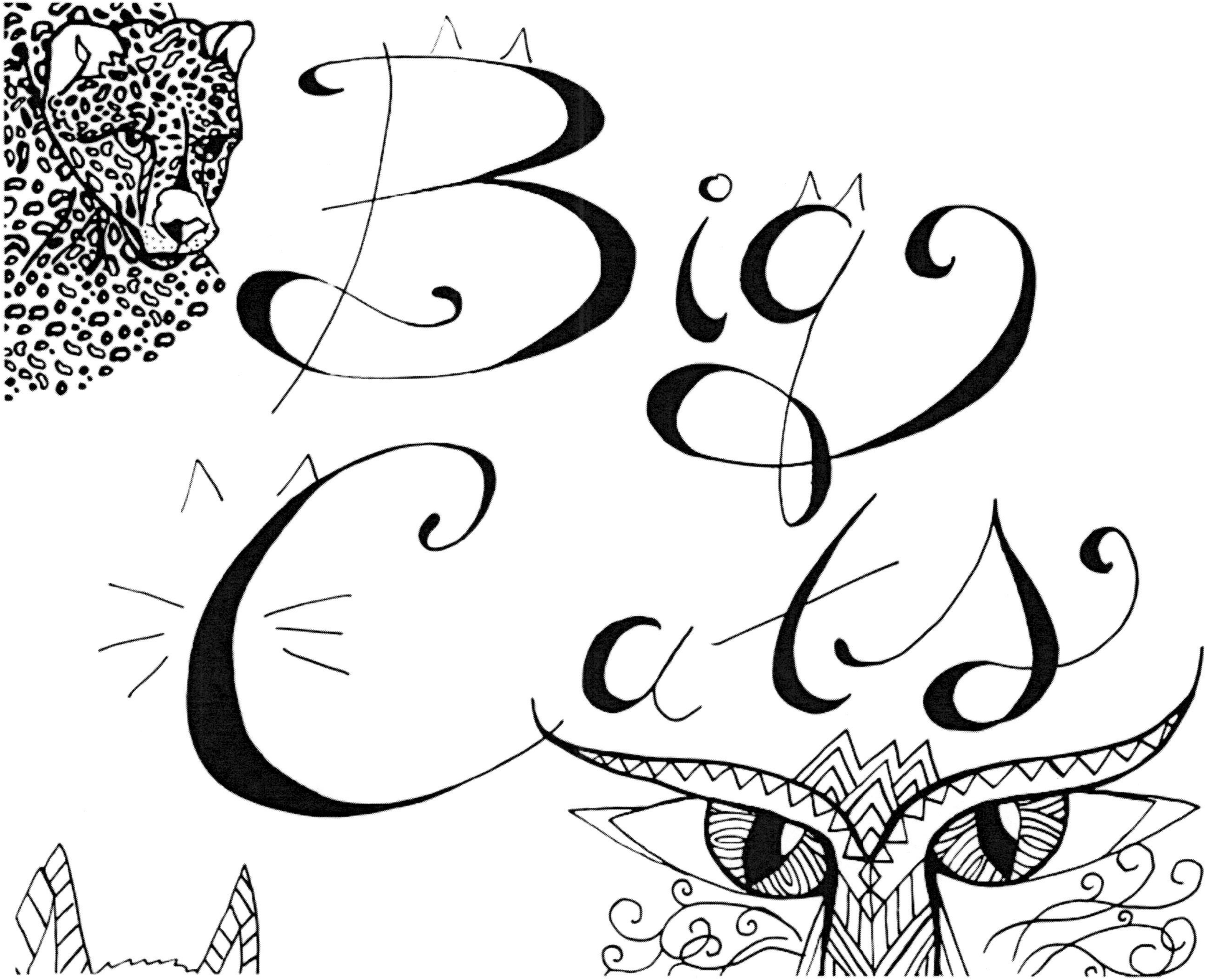
Big Cats

Panther

- **Fun Facts**
  - Panthers can generally be divided into two categories: Black Leopards and Jaguars.
  - Panthers are melanistic, meaning that they have excessive dark pigmentation. Being melanistic is the opposite of being albino.
  - Panthers actually have spots—they are just too dark to see against the rest of its nearly black coat.
  - A yellow leopard mother can have yellow and black cubs in the same litter.
  - Newborn panthers are born with their eyes closed.
  - After hunting a large animal, a panther will often still have enough strength to lift it up and carry it up a tree.
  - Panthers are highly adaptable creatures that are opportunistic hunters.
  - Panthers can run up to 36 miles per hour.
- **What do they Eat?**
  - Panthers eat deer, wild boar, tapir, antelope, warthogs, rabbits, and birds.
- **Where They Hang Out**
  - Panthers are native to North America, South Asia, and Africa.
- **Helpful Organization**
  - Florida Panther Protection Program

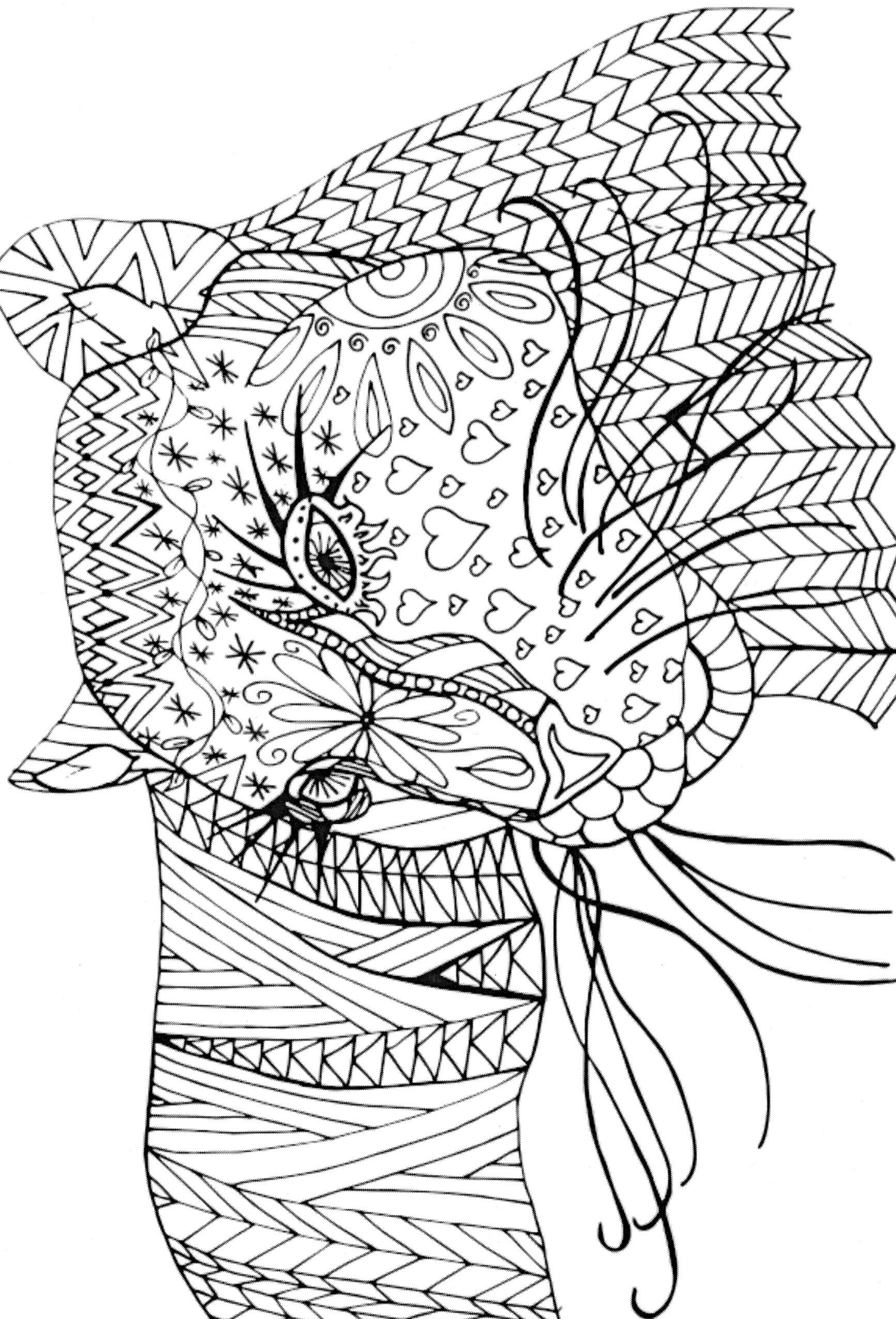

Cheetah

- **Fun Facts**
  - Cheetahs are antisocial animals. The females raise their cubs by themselves and males occasionally spend time with a small group of brothers from the same litter.
  - Cheetahs cannot roar. They actually purr like house cats.
  - A mother cheetah will have between 2-4 cubs in each litter. Cheetah cubs are gray with long, wool-like hair.
  - Cheetahs use their tail to steer themselves when they are running—much like the rudder on a boat.
  - Cheetahs are the fastest known land animal in the world. They can reach their top speed, (almost 80 mph), within 3 seconds flat. This is partially because they are fairly light, they have large lungs and wide nostrils, and are aerodynamic in shape.
  - Cheetahs are able to turn mid-air while they are sprinting...so they are basically furry ninjas.
- **What do they Eat?**
  - Cheetahs survive by hunting gazelles, impalas, small hoofed animals, and young wildebeests.
- **Where They Hang Out**
  - Cheetahs live in Savannahs throughout South Africa, India, and Asia.
- **Helpful Organization**
  - Cheetah Conservation Fund

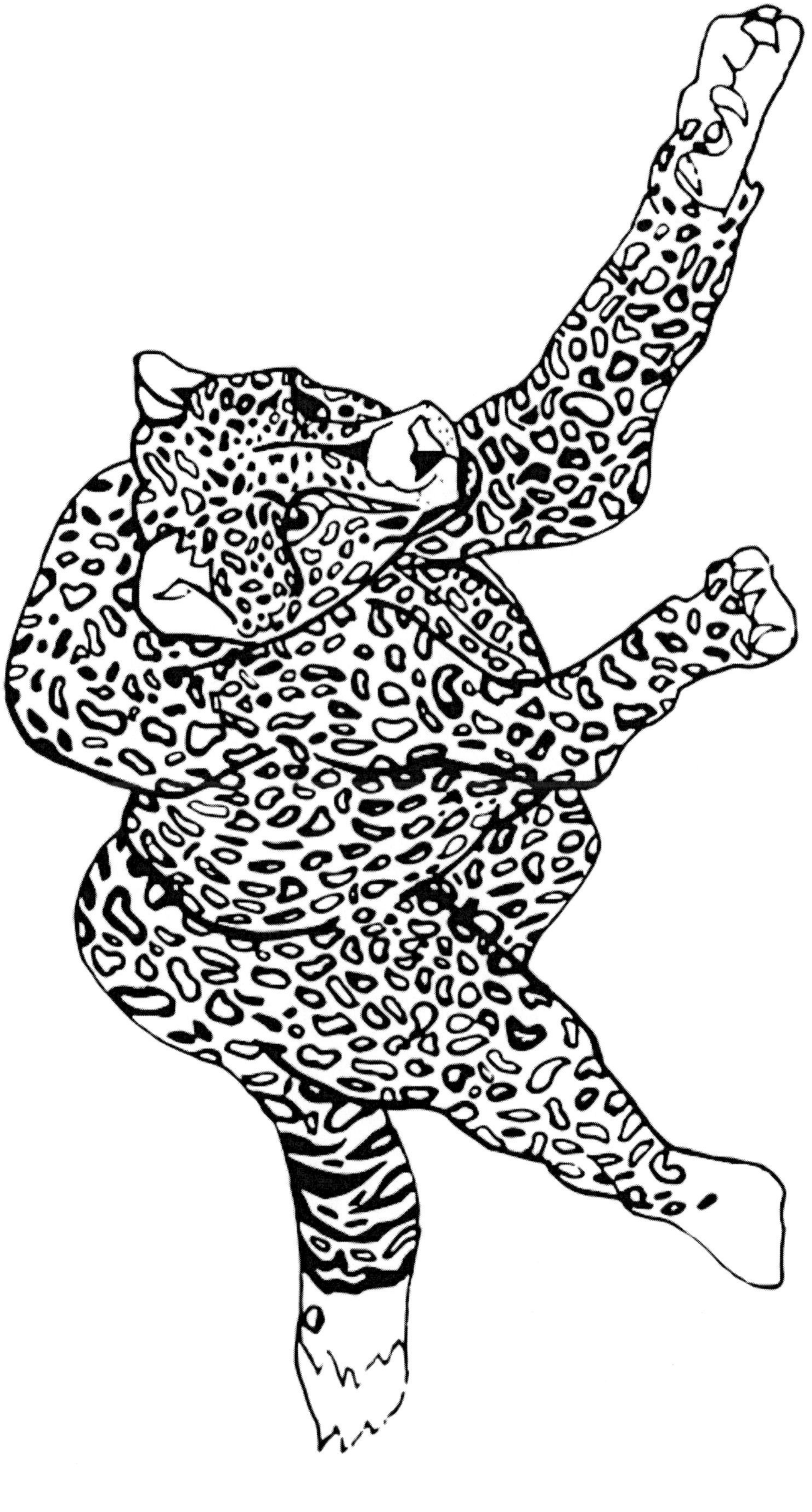

Tigers

- **Fun Facts**
  - Tigers are antisocial creatures that spend most of their time alone. They are very territorial and scent-mark large territories. No two tigers have the same set of stripes.
  - A tiger is capable of killing animals up to twice its size. If its prey is too large to move efficiently, a tiger will drag parts of it off and bury it loosely with leaves. It will return later for the rest. So, basically, tigers create little pantry holes for themselves.
  - Tigers are excellent swimmers and enjoy cooling off in lakes and streams when it's hot out.
  - Tigers rely heavily on their teeth for survival. If a tiger loses its canines, it can no longer kill and will probably starve to death.
  - A tiger cub cannot hunt until it is at least 18 months old.
- **What do they Eat?**
  - Tigers eat game animals, wild boar, monkeys, lizards, and porcupines.
- **Where They Hang Out**
  - Tigers can be found throughout South-East Asia, Korea, China, and Russia.
- **Helpful Organization**
  - Save the Tiger Fund

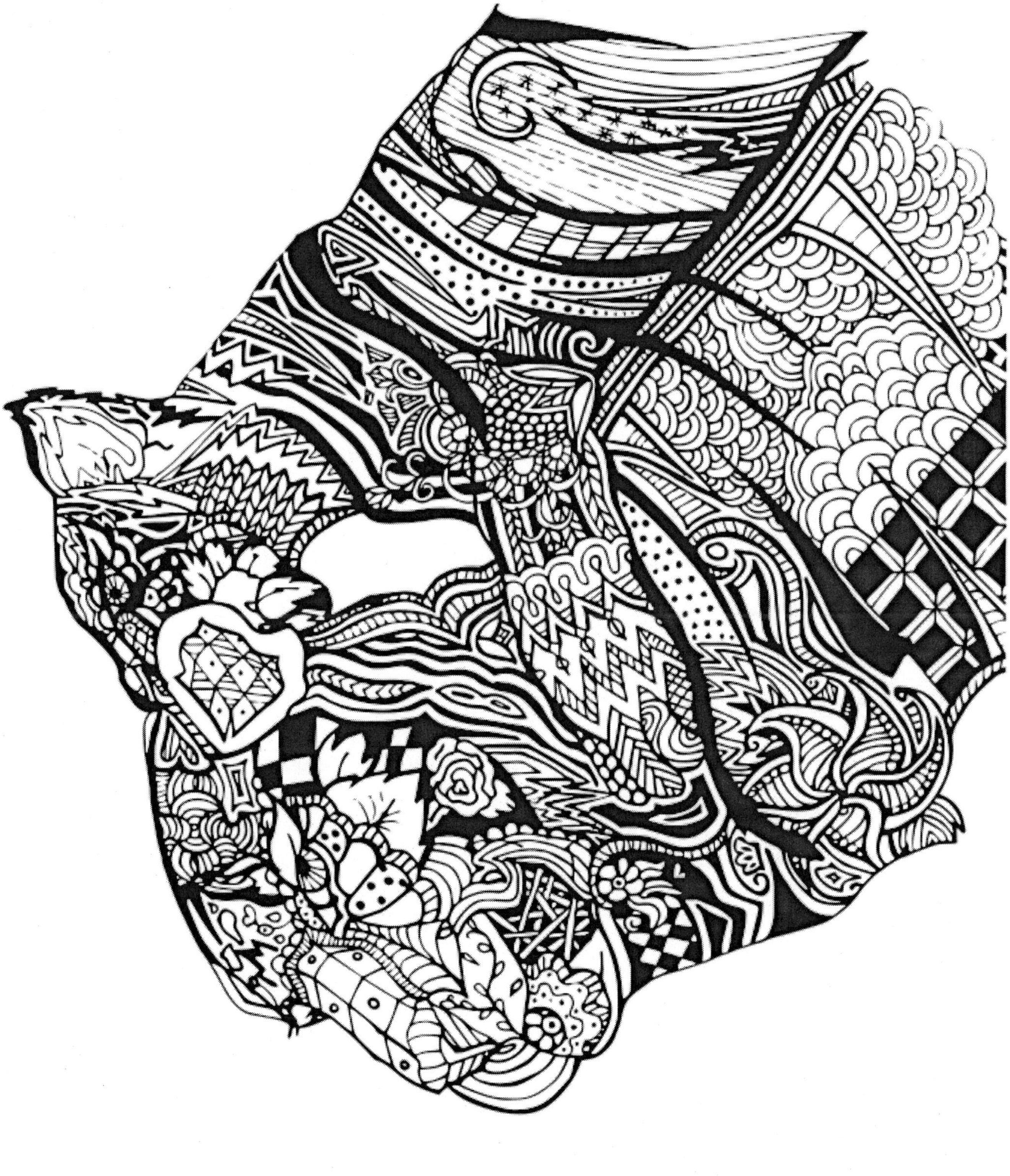

Lions

- **Fun Facts**
  - The African Lion grows to be about 4-7 feet long from its head to its bottom and its tail measures measures between 26-40 inches long. African lions weigh between 260 and 420 lbs.
  - The Asian Lion can grow up to 9 feet long and can weigh between 300 and 500 pounds.
  - Only male lions can grow manes around their heads. Manes help males look more intimidating and also help protect the lion's head during fights over territories.
  - Lions are very social. They live in large groups called prides which, for African Lions, consist of 3 males and 12 females and their cubs. Asian Lions have segregated prides according to gender. Male and female prides only meet up for mating purposes.
  - Male lions often run off to create their own prides. Female lions usually remain loyal to one pride their whole lives.
- **What do they Eat?**
  - African Lions eat wildebeests, antelope, and zebras. Asiatic Lions eat buffaloes, goats, nilgai, and chital.
- **Where They Hang Out**
  - Lions can be found throughout Africa, Asia, and Europe.
- **Helpful Organization**
  - Lion Conservation Fund

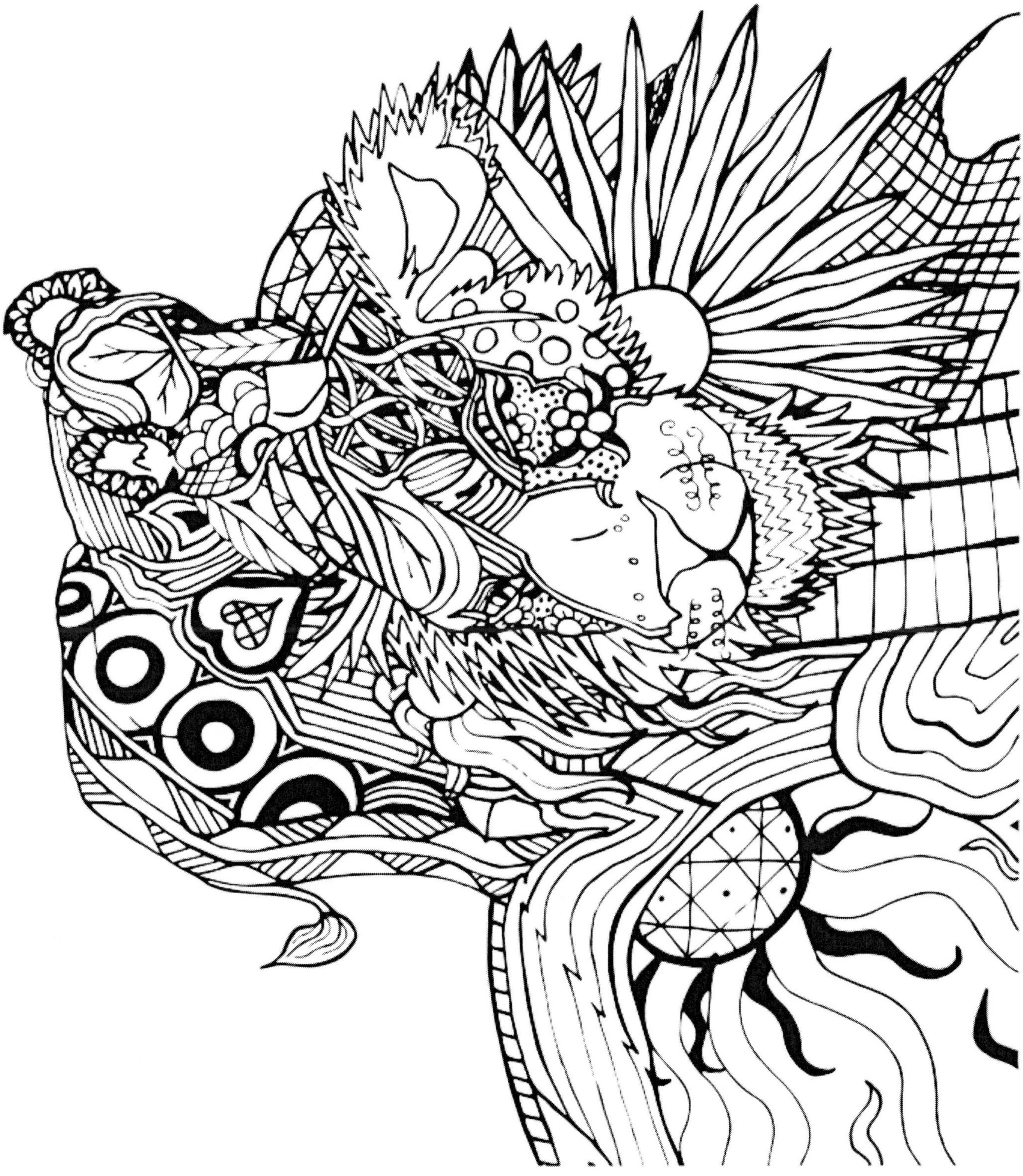

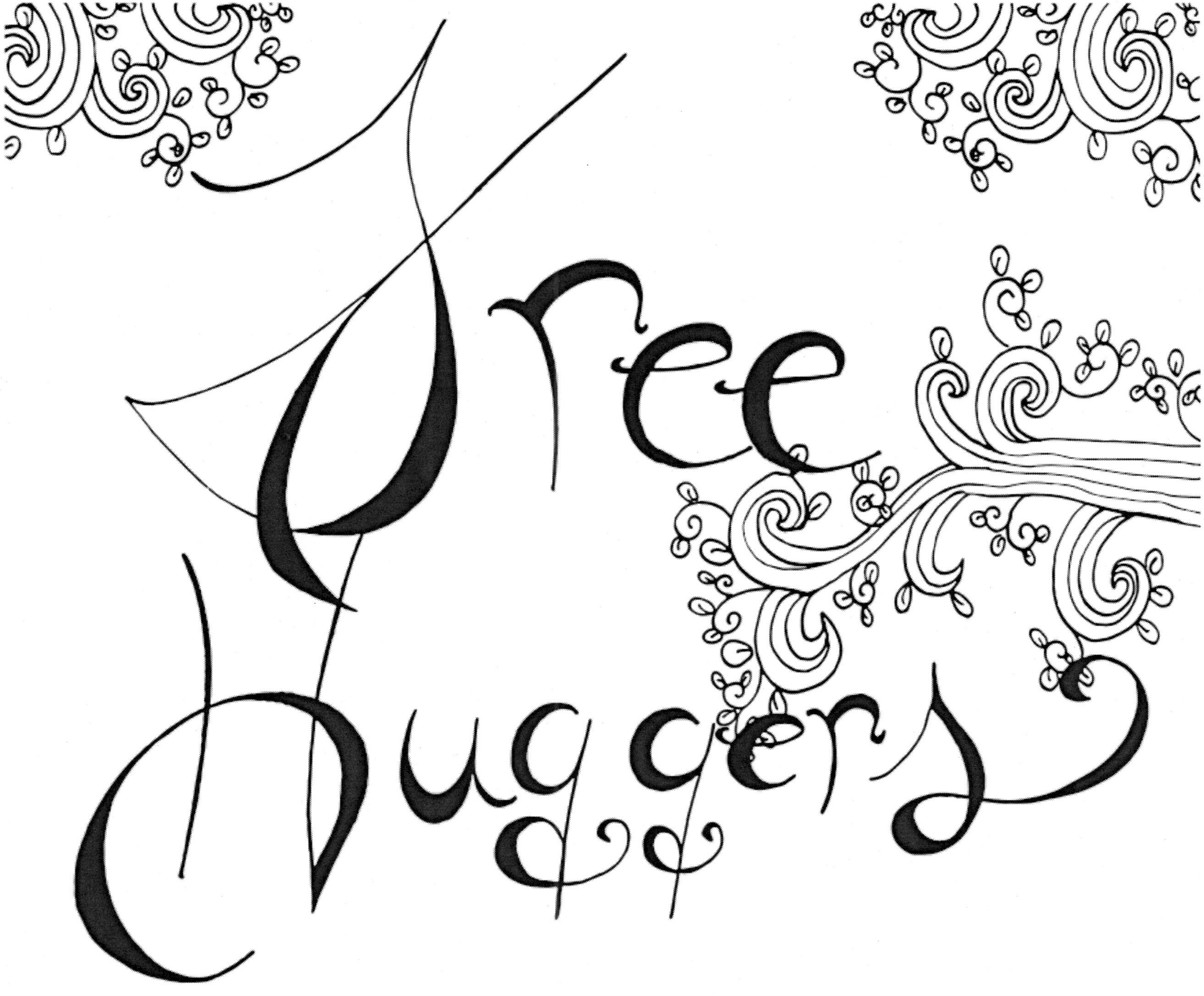
Tree Huggers

Chimpanzees

- **Fun Facts**
  - We share 98% of our DNA with chimps.
  - Chimpanzees are very social creatures. They have a fission-fusion society of 15-20 members, where each of them know one another but they tend to split off into smaller groups of 6 or less in order to travel, feed and sleep. Sometimes, they will swap members of these smaller social circles.
  - Chimps will sometimes have large gatherings where more than half of their society will show up. These are social events.
  - Chimps maintain a patriarchal hierarchy, although the alpha's status depends largely upon how much support he gets from the females in the group.
  - Chimps communicate through a complex vocal language, facial expressions, and gestures.
- **What do they Eat?**
  - Chimps are omnivorous, eating mostly fruits, leaves, insects, eggs, nuts, bark, and smaller animals. They even eat some other monkey species.
- **Where They Hang Out**
  - Chimpanzees are native to Africa.
- **Helpful Organization**
  - Save the Chimps

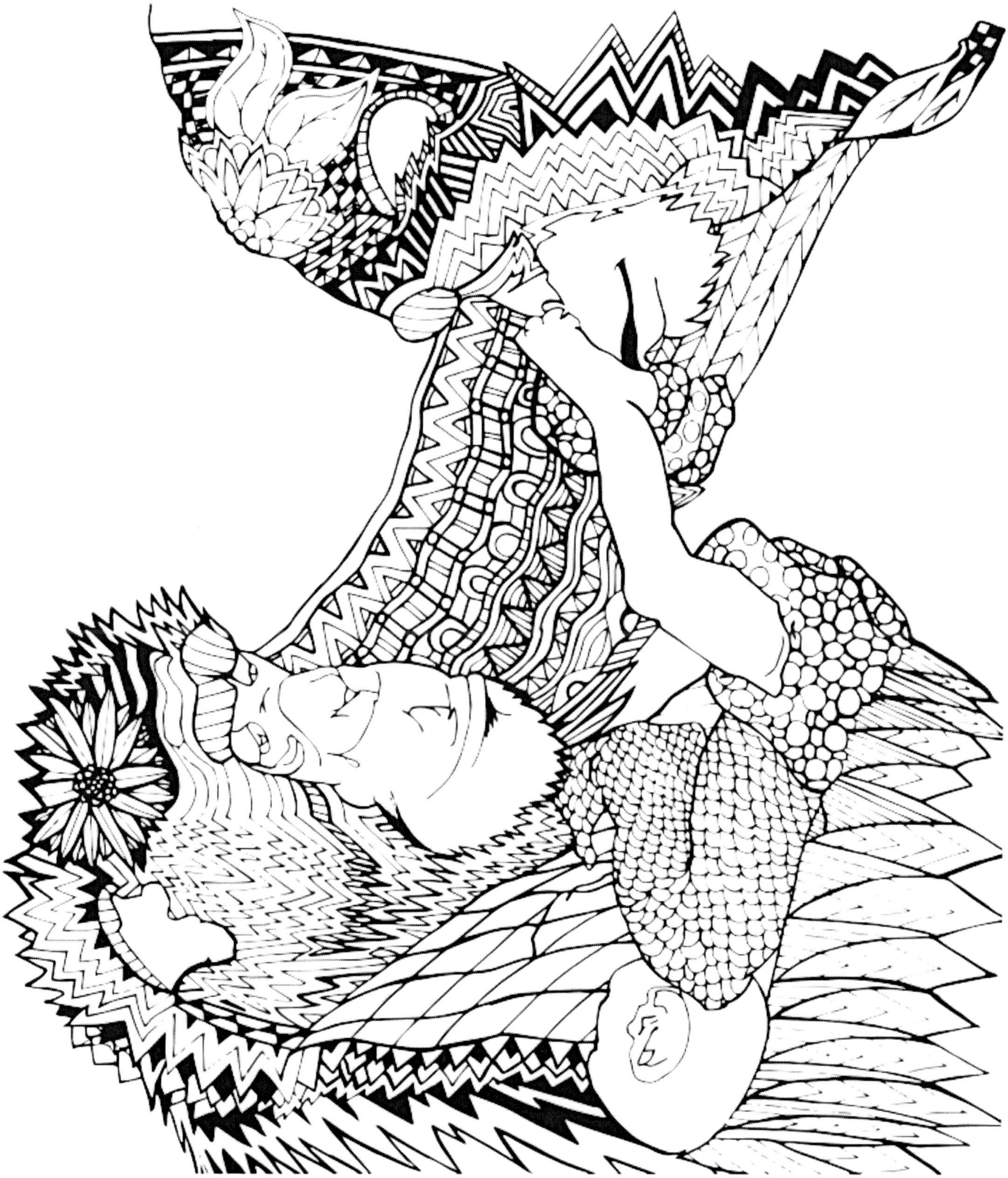

Spider Monkey

- **Fun Facts**
  - Spider Monkeys are very social animals. They are generally found in large groups of up to three dozen members. When they sleep, they create smaller sleeping parties of about 5-6 monkeys.
  - Mothers give birth to one spider monkey every two to five years.
  - Unlike most monkeys, spider monkeys do not have opposing thumbs.
  - Spider Monkeys have very long prehensile tails that are sometimes used as a fifth limb.
  - Spider Monkeys are, on average, 3-5 feet tall and can live to be 22-25 years old in the wild.
  - When spider monkeys hang from trees, they spread out their limbs and hold different branches. When they do this, they resemble spiders and spider webs and that's how they earned their names.
  - Spider monkeys are almost never on the ground. They live, breed, eat, sleep, and give birth up in trees.
- **What do they Eat?**
  - Spider Monkeys eat fruits, spiders, bird eggs, leaves, insects and nuts.
- **Where They Hang Out**
  - Spider Monkeys spend most of their days up in the lush canopies of tropical rainforests throughout Central America, South America, and Mexico.
- **Helpful Organization**
  - Spider Monkey Conservation Project

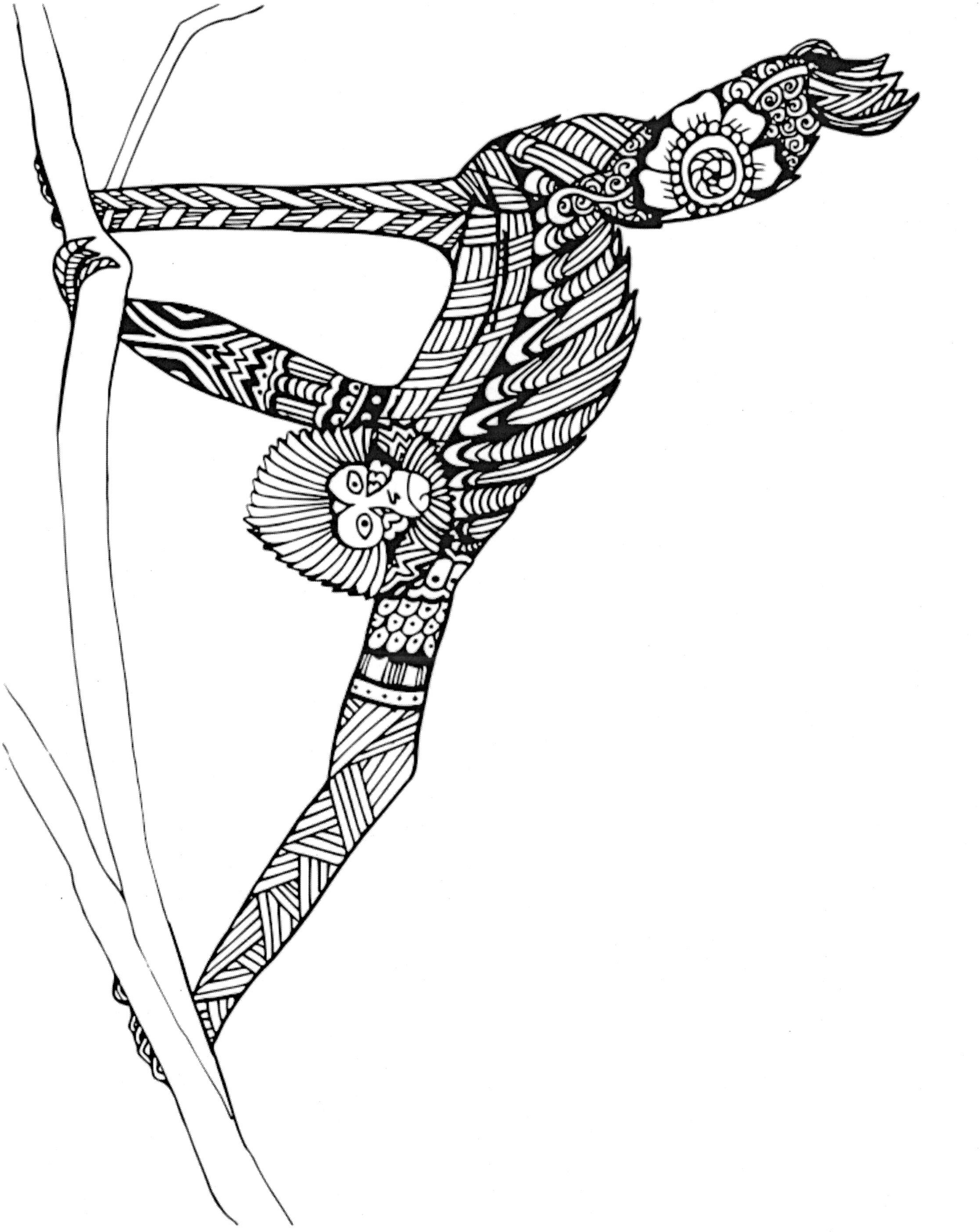

Koala

- **Fun Facts**
  - Koalas are actually not bears at all. They are marsupials.
  - Female koalas have pouches (not unlike that of a kangaroo) where their children stay during youth.
  - Koalas have an extra thick layer of fur on their bottoms and a pad of cartilage at the base of their spines. This makes it more comfortable for them to sit on tree branches.
  - Koalas have curved spines and have two fewer ribs than other mammals.
  - Koalas are incredibly territorial. They mark their boundaries with a sticky brown secretion that comes from a scent gland in their chests. They rub this stuff on the bark of trees to outline their home range.
  - A baby koala is referred to as a *joey*.
  - Koalas live to be around 10 to 15 years old.
- **What do they Eat?**
  - Koala bears mainly survive on eucalyptus leaves.
- **Where They Hang Out**
  - Orcas prefer cold, coastal waters, although they can be seen everywhere from the poles to the equator.
- **Helpful Organization**
  - The Australian Koala Foundation

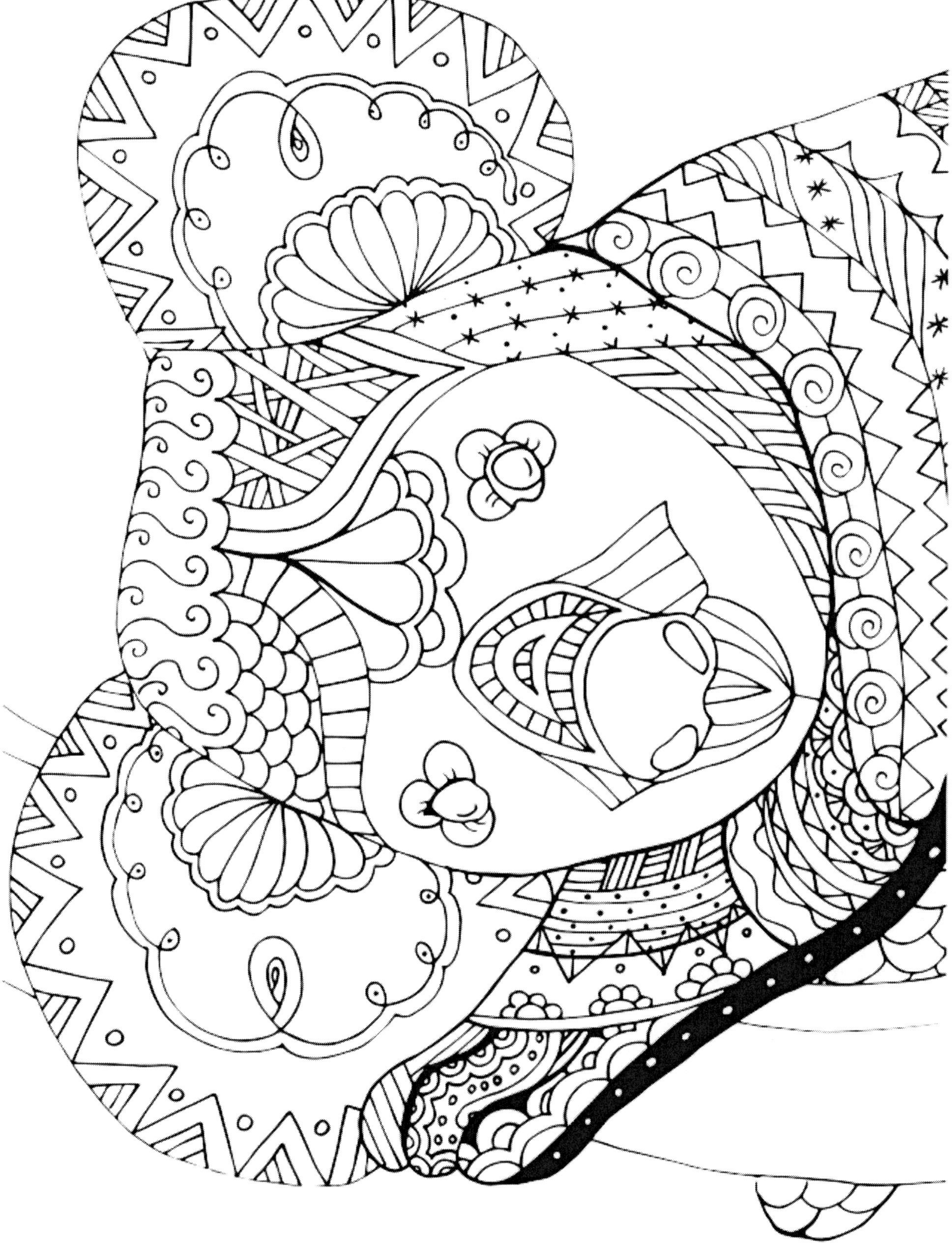

3-Toed Sloths

- **Fun Facts**
  - Sloths are the world's slowest moving animal. They are so, well, sloth-like that algae grows on their fur, giving them a greenish tint that helps them camouflage up in the trees.
  - Sloths sleep between 15 and 20 hours a day.
  - Sloths have extra neck vertebrae, allowing them to turn their heads around 270 degrees.
  - Ancient sloths were huge. There are sloth skeletons dating back thousands of years that are as large as elephants.
  - Sloths hardly eat at all. Because they digest slowly and have a 4-part stomach, they can survive on one single meal for up to a whole month.
  - While they mostly love to climb trees, sloths are also fantastic swimmers. It's not uncommon for them to high-dive off of a tree branch and into some water.
- **What do they Eat?**
  - Sloths mostly eat leaves.
- **Where They Hang Out**
  - Sloths are generally found in South, Central, and North America.
- **Helpful Organization**
  - Pygmy Three-Toed Sloth Conservation

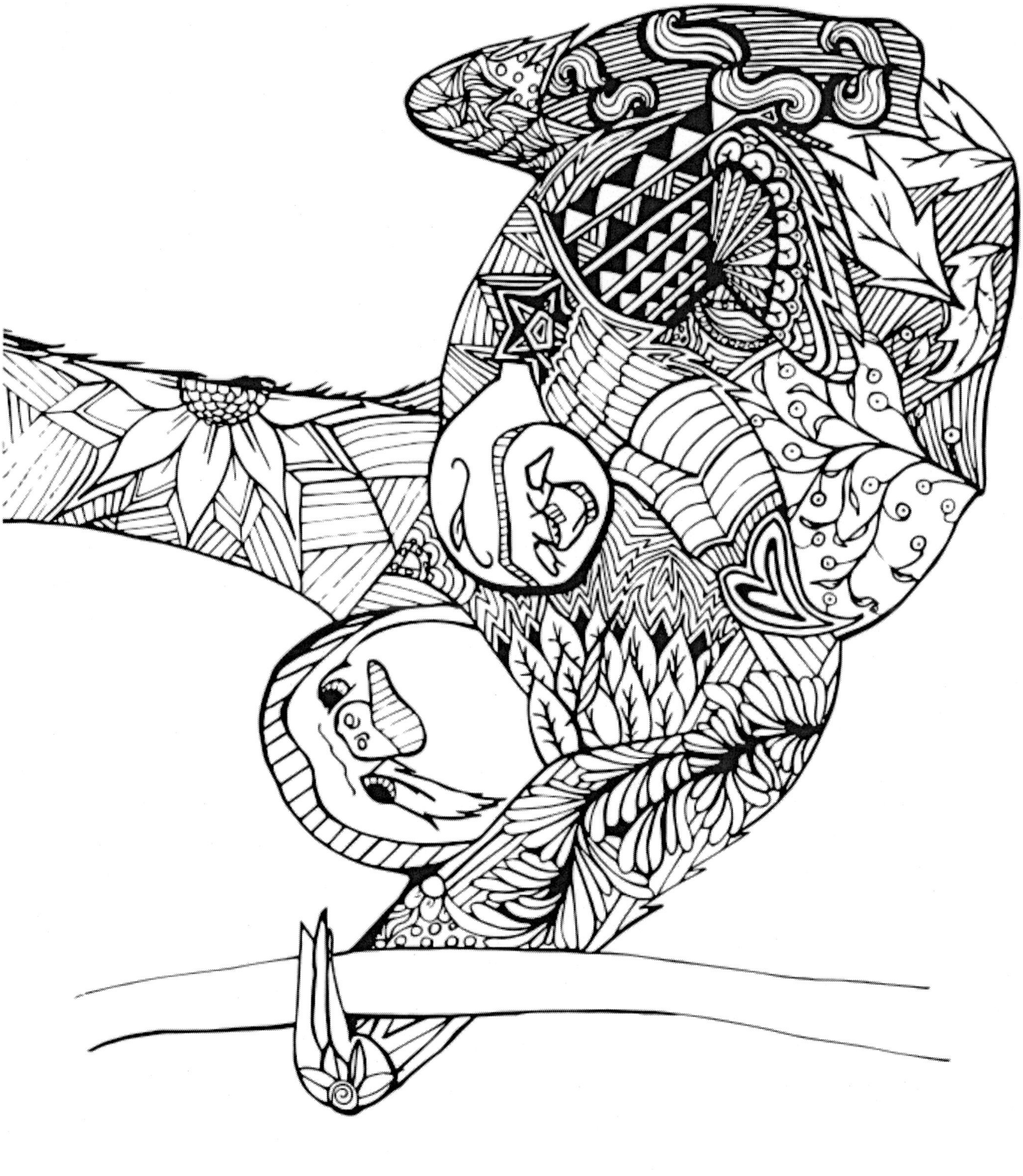

Exotic Beasts

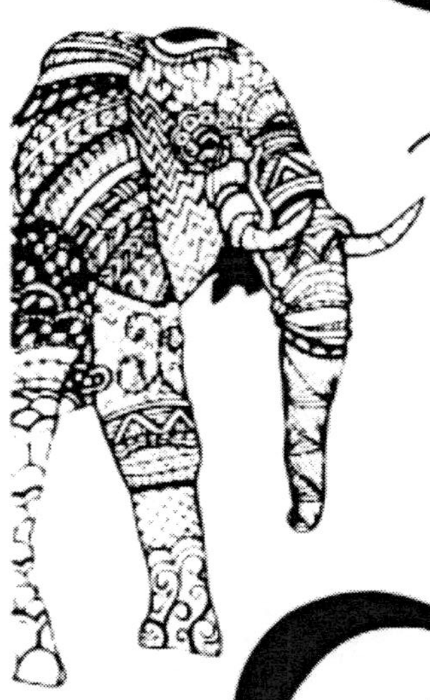

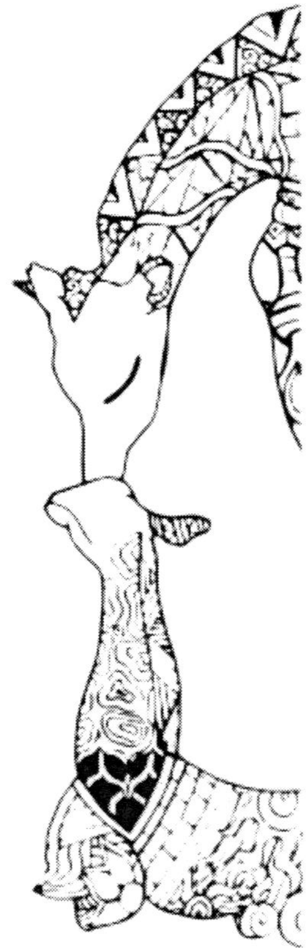

Rhinoceros

- **Fun Facts**
  - Mother rhinoceroses care for their young for up to 4 years.
  - Rhinoceroses are temperamental, especially in areas where they are hunted regularly for their horns.
  - A rhino's horn is actually not skeletal at all. It's made from keratin and thickly matted hair that spirals upward.
  - In Asia, rhinoceroses are often hunted for their horns, which are either carved for decoration or used in traditional medicines.
  - There are five different species of rhinoceroses.
  - Rhinoceroses can grow up to 6 feet tall and 11 feet in length.
  - While rhinos have very thick skin, it's actually particularly sensitive, particularly to insect bites and sunburns.
  - *White Rhinoceroses* and *Black Rhinoceroses* are all actually gray.
- **What do they Eat?**
  - Black rhinoceroses eat leaves, buds and shoots of plants, and bushes. White rhinoceroses graze on grasses.
- **Where They Hang Out**
  - White rhinoceroses live in Savannas and grasslands. Black rhinoceroses live in dense, wooded areas.
- **Helpful Organization**
  - Save the Rhino

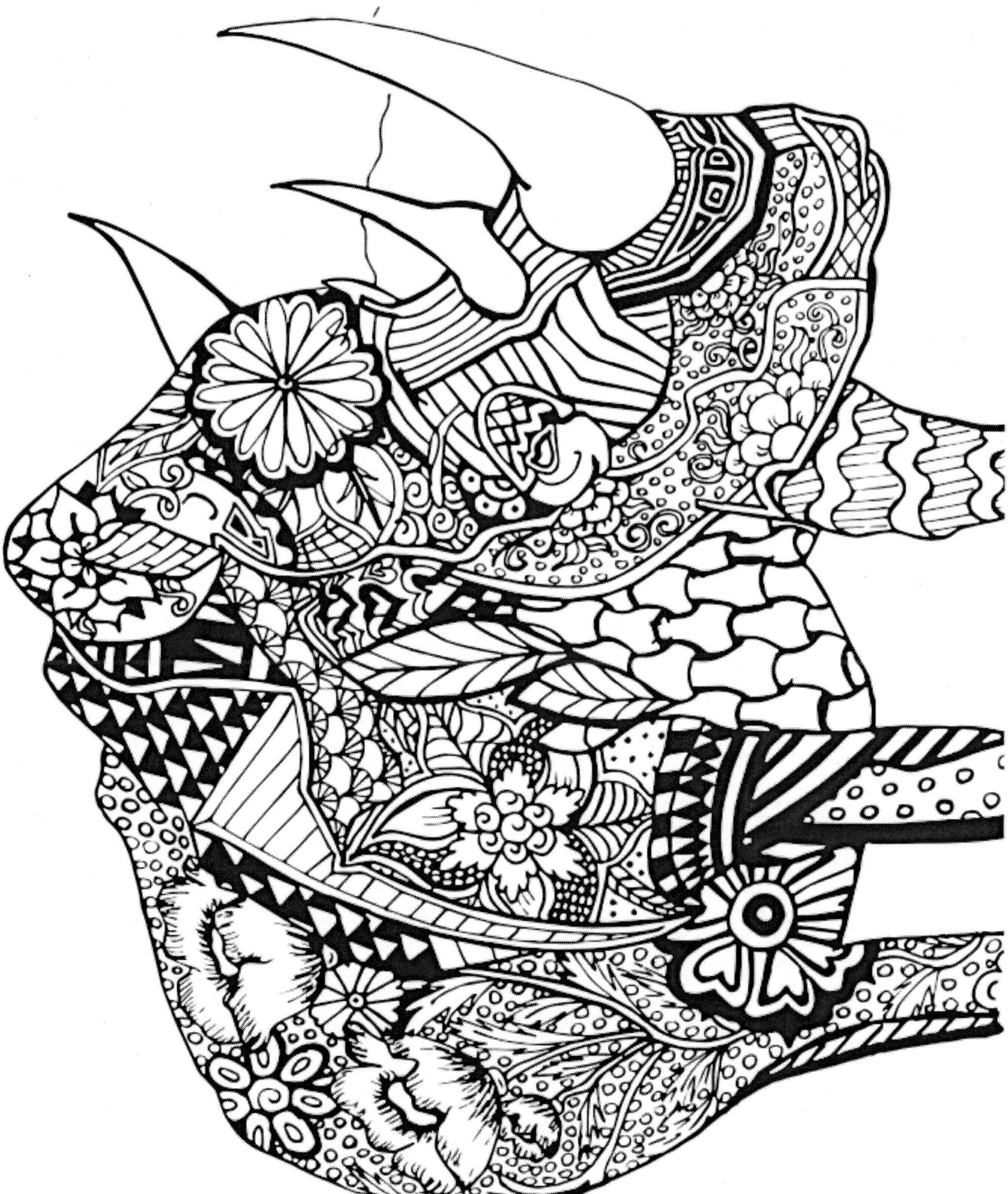

Zebra

- **Fun Facts**
  - A Zebra's stripes are completely unique to him or her. In a sense, they act as really beautiful fingerprints.
  - While these stripes are different for each individual, patterns turn up within each of the three Zebra species.
  - Zebras are very social. They spend most of their time in herds called *harems* and rely on one another for protection.
  - Zebras are born whie and brown. It isn't until they grow older that their brown stripes darken to black.
  - Every Zebra is fairly attached to his or her mother, but male Zebras also tend to form really strong bonds with their fathers, too.
  - Zebras have solid black skin beneath their striped coats—an unusual trait for striped animals.
  - Zebras can run up to 65 km/hr and evade predators by running in confusing zigzag patterns.
- **What do they Eat?**
  - Zebras graze on grass, herbs, twigs, shrubs, leaves and bark.
- **Where They Hang Out**
  - Zebras can be found in the Savannas throughout Zimbabwe, Namibia, Angola and Kenya.
- **Helpful Organization**
  - African Wildlife Foundation

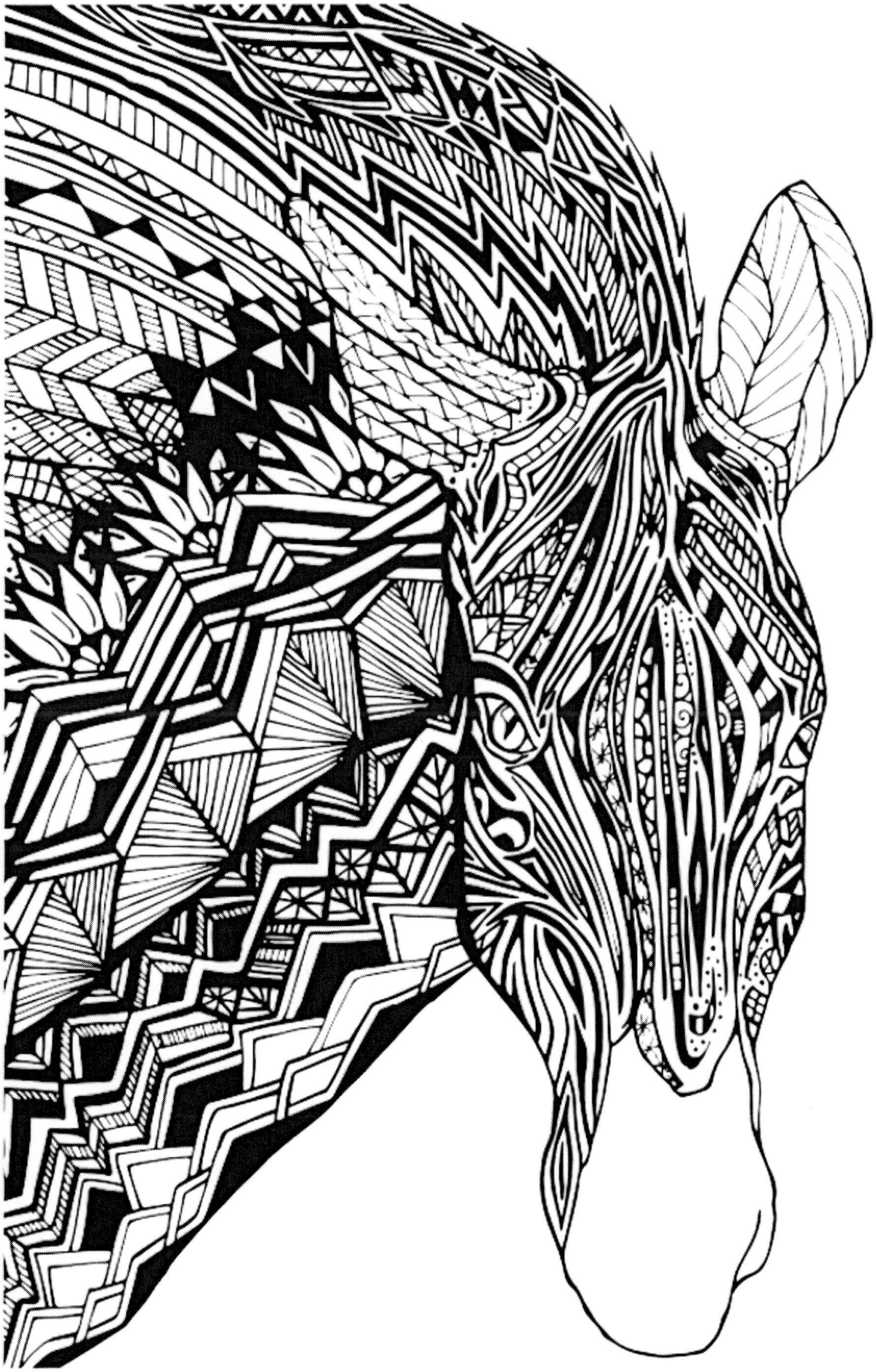

Giant Pandas

- **Fun Facts**
    - Giant Pandas can grow up to 4 to 5 feet tall. Their distant cousins, *Red Pandas,* are only 20-26 inches tall.
    - There are currently only about 1,600 Giant Pandas out in the wild and only about 100 living in zoos.
    - They are considered a national treasure in China.
    - Giant Pandas are antisocial. If they smell another panda coming near, they leave abruptly so they don't have to interact with it.
    - Pandas mark their territory by secreting a waxy scent. Generally, a panda will try to maintain a territory of about 2 square miles.
    - The scent that they secrete also informs other pandas of the sex, social status, age and reproductive condition of that panda.
- **What do they Eat?**
    - Giant Pandas eat rodents, fish, insects, birds, and bamboo. They snack on bamboo for up to 12 hours a day, consuming more than 28 pounds of the stuff.
- **Where They Hang Out**
    - Giant Pandas are native to China, where they live in wet bamboo forests.
- **Helpful Organization**
    - Giant Panda Conservation Fund

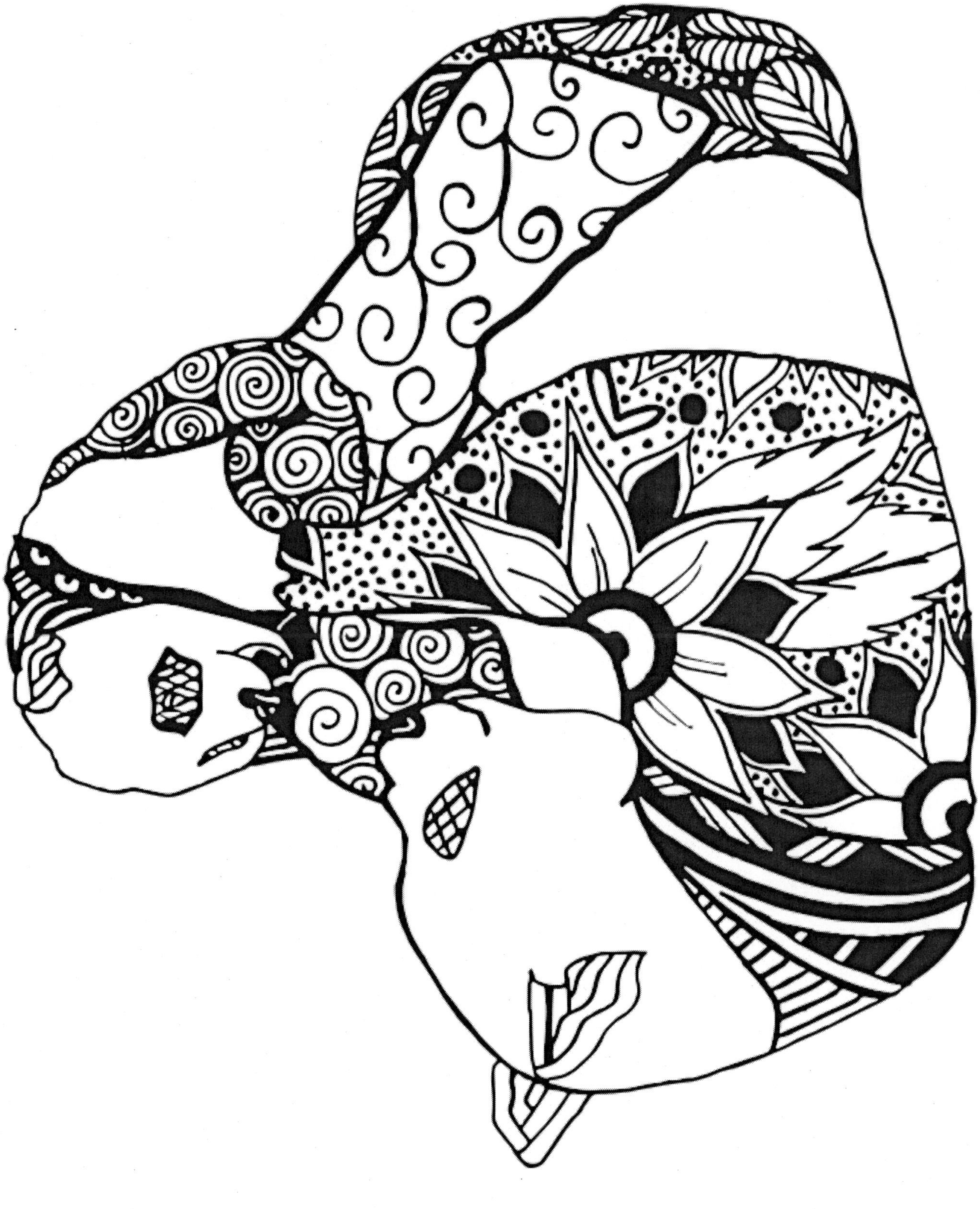

Kangaroos

- **Fun Facts**
  - There are four species of kangaroos.
  - Male kangaroos are called *boomers, bucks,* or *jacks.* Female kangaroos are known as *does, flyers,* or *jills*. When they are young, kangaroos are called *joeys*.
  - In order to move at a slower speed, a kangaroo will use its tail as a third limb. It then performs something called *crawl-walking*, whereby it raises its hind feet forward while balancing on its two front limbs and tail.
  - Kangaroos give birth to one joey at a time. The joey will stay in its mother's pouch for up to a year, depending on the species.
  - The smallest kangaroo is the *musky rat-kangaroo*. It measures a mere 6-8 inches long and weighs 12 ounces. The largest kangaroo is the *red kangaroo*. It grows up to 5 feet tall and can weigh over 200 pounds.
- **What do they Eat?**
  - Kangaroos are herbivores. For the most part they eat grass.
- **Where They Hang Out**
  - Kangaroos live in the grassy plains, forests, and woodland areas of Australia and Tasmania. They are also sometimes spotted throughout the neighboring islands.
- **Helpful Organization**
  - The Tree Kangaroo Conservation Program

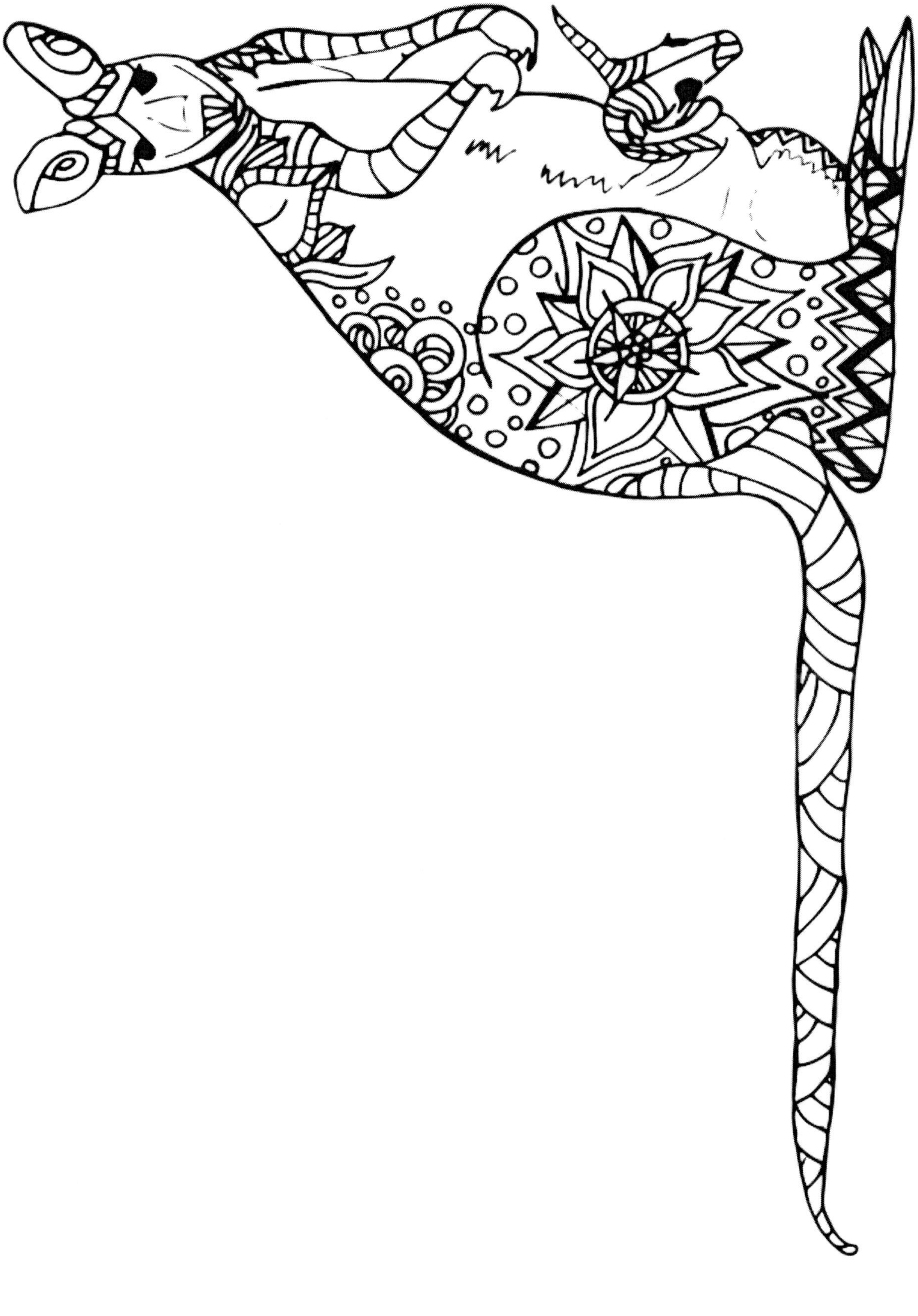

Anteater

- **Fun Facts**
  - The Latin term for anteaters, *Vermilingua,*translates to "worm tongue."
  - There are four different species of anteaters, but the most commonly known is the *Giant Anteater.*
  - Anteaters don't have teeth, but their tongues can reach out to more than the length of the head. In the case of the *Giant Anteater,*that means the tongue can extend out more than two feet.
  - Anteaters walk on their knuckles because their claws are long, non-retractable, and curved in.
  - The *Giant Anteater* has to eat up to 200 times a day just to survive.
  - An anteater's tongue is covered in a sticky saliva and thousands of tiny hooks.
  - An anteater can flick its tongue up to 150 times a minute.
  - Anteaters are very quiet, creating sounds only when threatening another male or during a fight.
- **What do they Eat?**
  - Anteaters eat termites, ants, fruits, and other small insects.
- **Where They Hang Out**
  - Anteaters can be found throughout Central and South America.
- **Helpful Organization**
  - Giant Anteater Conservation Project

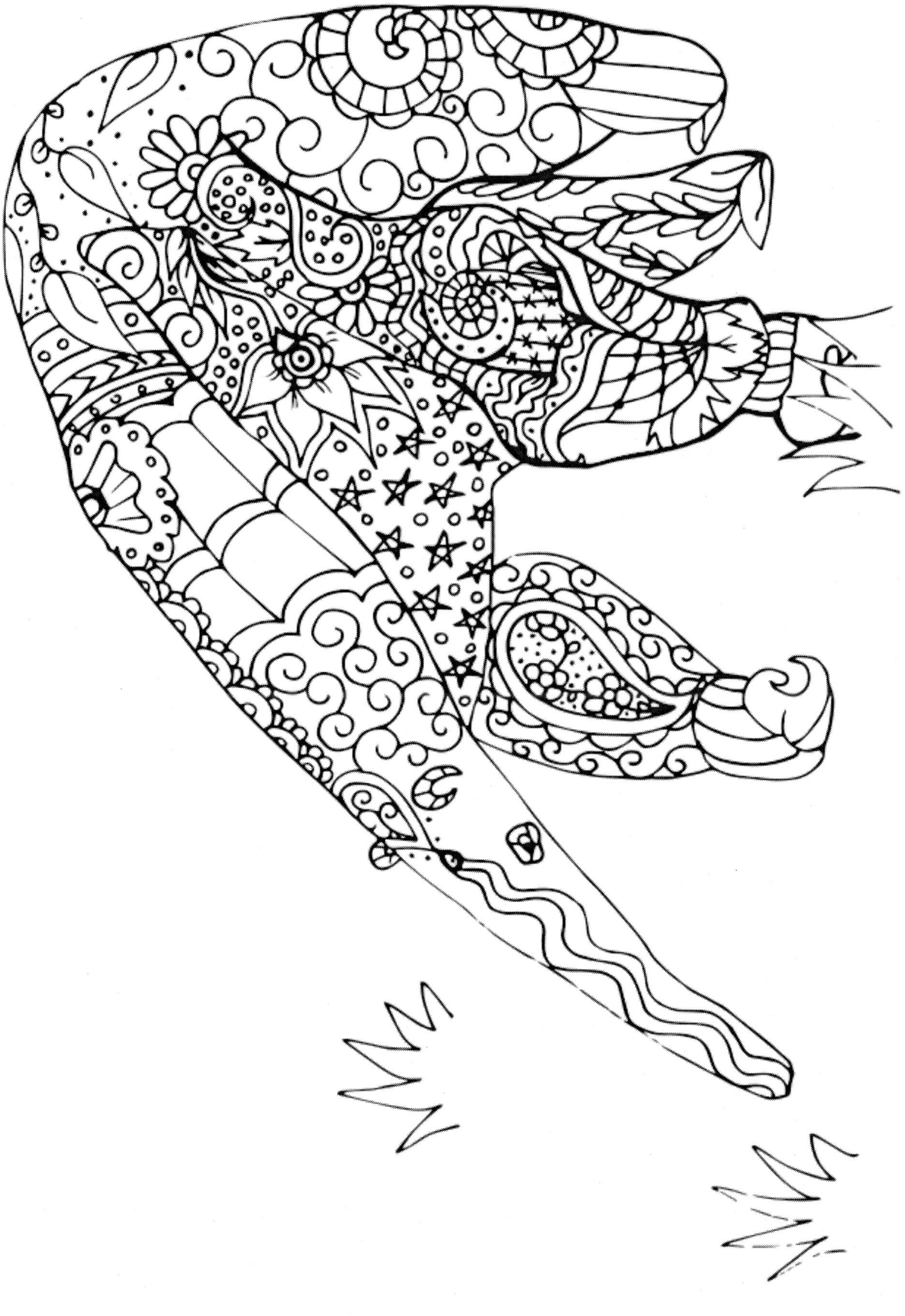

Giraffes

- **Fun Facts**
  - Giraffes are the tallest animal in the world, averaging about 16-18 feet.
  - A full-grown giraffe spends most of its day eating, consuming over 100 lbs of leaves and twigs a day.
  - When giraffes walk, they move both legs on one side of their body simultaneously and then do the same on the other side.
  - The skin covered knobs atop their heads helps protect them when in fights.
  - When giraffes fight, they swing their necks at one another. This is called *necking*.
  - Giraffes sleep less than two hours a day.
  - Female giraffes carry their young for 15 months and give birth while standing upright.
  - Giraffes live up to 25 years old in the wild.
- **What do they Eat?**
  - Giraffes are herbivorous, surviving on leaves and shoots that they find high up in tree canopies.
- **Where They Hang Out**
  - Giraffes mainly live in savannah areas in sub-Saharan Africa.
- **Helpful Organization**
  - Giraffe Conservation Foundation

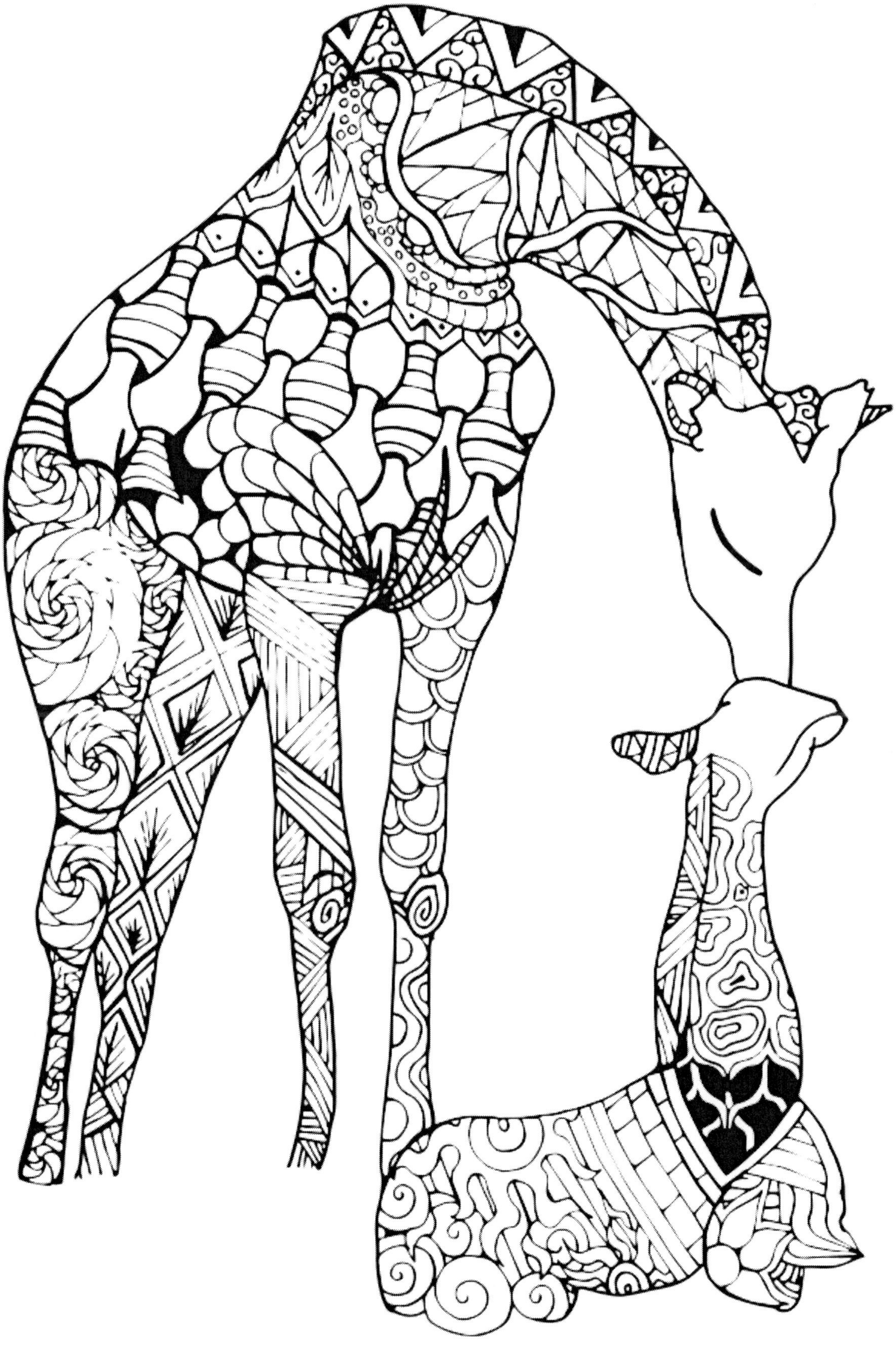

Elephant

- **Fun Facts**
  - Adult elephants eat between 300 and 400 lbs of food a day.
  - Female Elephants live in matriarchal families called *herds*. They are highly emotional and maintain strong bonds with their family members. When they are between 12 and 15 years old, male elephants will leave the herd and live solitary lives.
  - Elephants are highly intelligent and emotive creatures. They have excellent memories and show signs of joy, anger, grief, and playfulness.
  - Elephants are able to communicate over long distances using sub-sonic rumbles that travel over the ground. They receive these messages through the sensitive skin on their feet and trunks.
  - Generally, a mother will only birth one elephant at a time, although they will sometimes have twins.
- **What do they Eat?**
  - Elephants eat leaves, grass, bamboo, roots, bark, banana crops, and sugarcane.
- **Where They Hang Out**
  - Elephants can be divided into two species, depending on where they live. African Elephants live throughout Central, South, and West Africa. Asian Elephants live throughout India, Sri-Lanka, Southeast Asia, and China.
- **Helpful Organization**
  - International Elephant Foundation

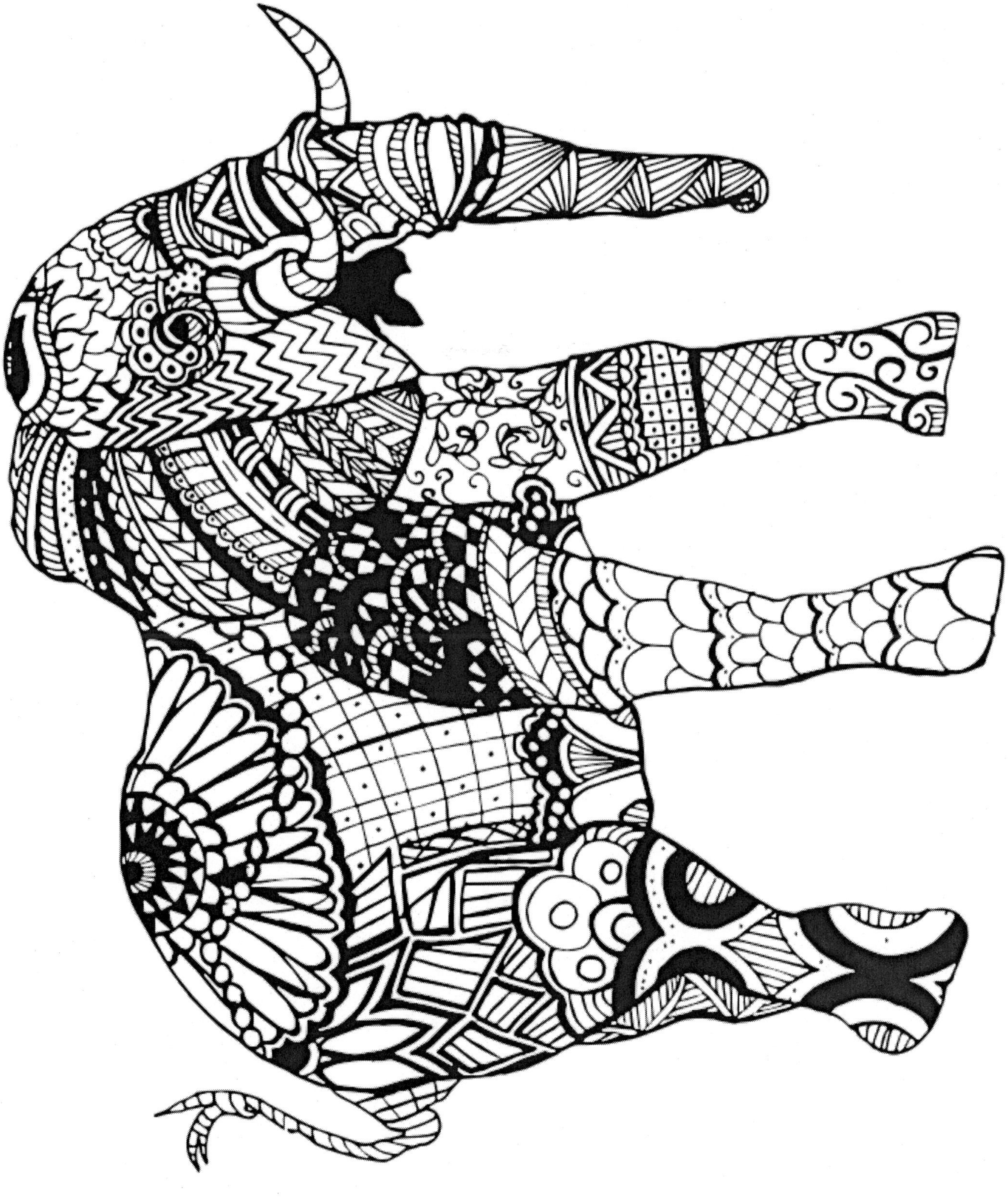

Scurrying Critters

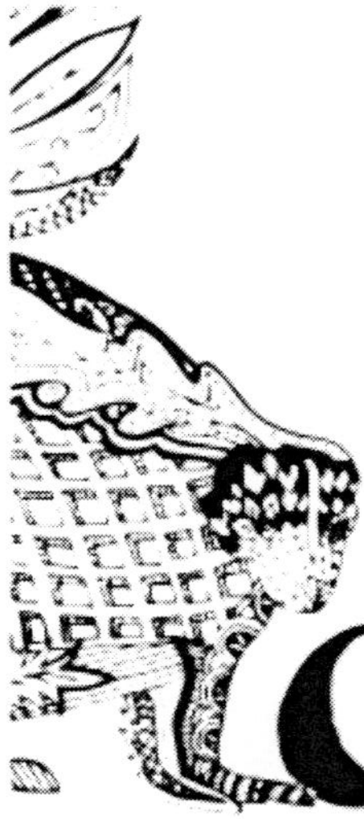

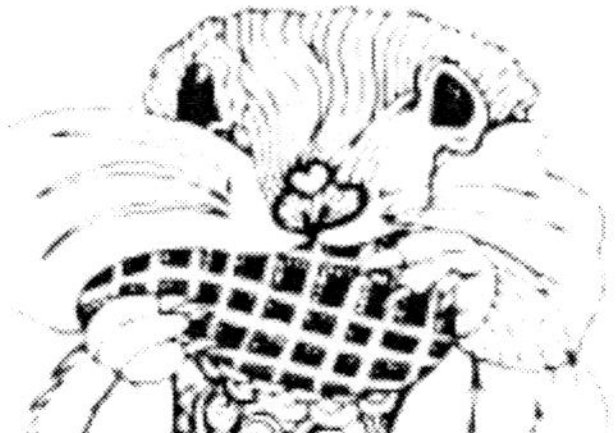

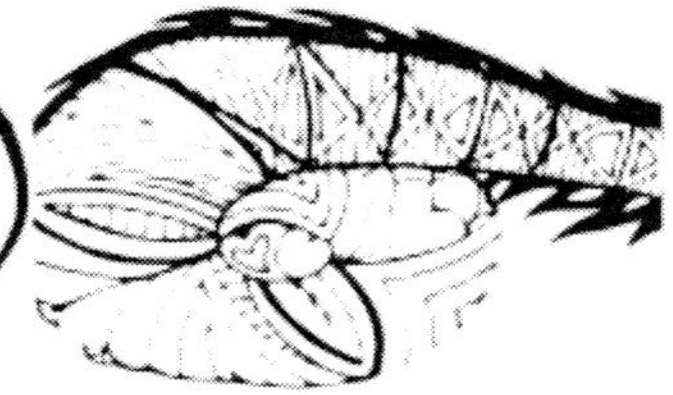

Mouse

- **Fun Facts**
    - Mice communicate both vocally, (sometimes on levels that human ears can't hear), and using odors. They can also communicate using facial expressions the way humans do.
    - Contrary to popular belief, mice are actually particularly clean creatures. They keep their homes organized and prefer tidy spaces to messy ones. Shamans use them to symbolize wisdom and organization.
    - Mice are also thought to empathize with one another. When they see a mouse that is sad, they feel sad as well.
    - Mice have incredible balance. They can tightrope walk across ropes and wires and can even climb up rough vertical surfaces. They are also acrobatic. They can jump down 3-4 meters without harming themselves.
- **What do they Eat?**
    - Mice are fond of carbohydrates like grains and seeds. They do, of course, enjoy cheese and are even attracted to chocolate and fruits.
- **Where They Hang Out**
    - Mice will live in almost any place imaginable. They love forests, will burrow underground, and will sneak into man-made structures.
- **Helpful Organization**
    - Center for Alternatives to Animal Testing

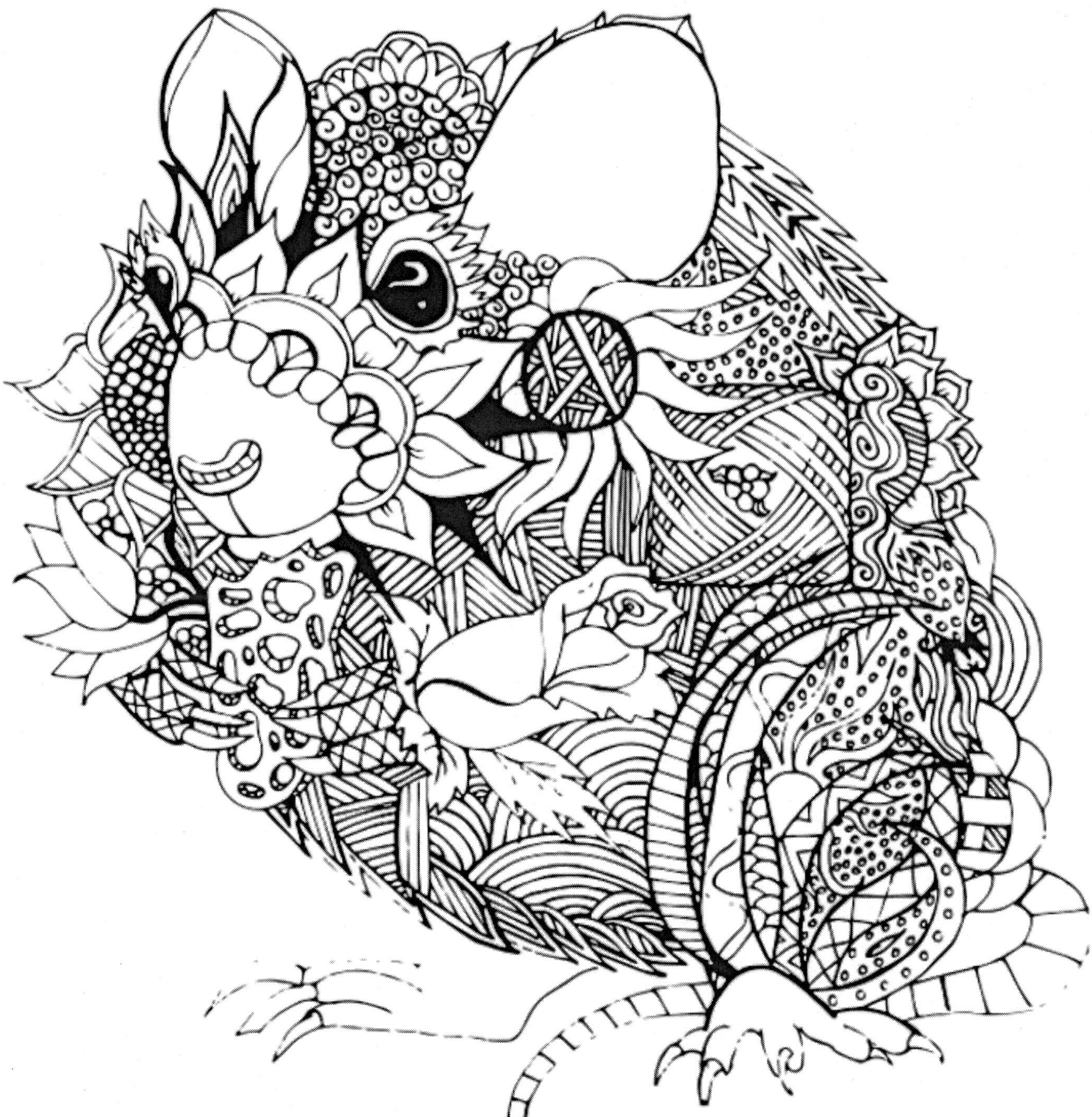

Raccoons

- **Fun Facts**
  - Raccoons have one to seven cubs early on in the summer.
  - Raccoons don't hibernate per se, but they do sleep for extended periods of time during the winter.
  - Raccoons are excellent swimmers.
  - Raccoons communicate with one another using 200 different sounds.
  - Raccoons keep their social circles small, forming close bonds with 4 to 5 individuals. They rely on one another for protection and help each other find food.
  - Raccoons are dexterous. They can open jars, latches, bottles, and doors. They are also adept at climbing.
  - In the wild, a raccoon's life span ranges between 1-3 years. When in captivity, that can extend up to 20 years.
- **What do they Eat?**
  - Raccoons are omnivorous and notorious for eating just about everything. They'll snag frogs, crayfish, mice, insects, birds' eggs, fruits, plants, and will even rummage through your trash.
- **Where They Hang Out**
  - Raccoons are found almost everywhere: they live near forests, marshes, prairies, and even in cities and suburban neighborhoods.
- **Helpful Organization**
  - Florida Fish and Wildlife Conservation

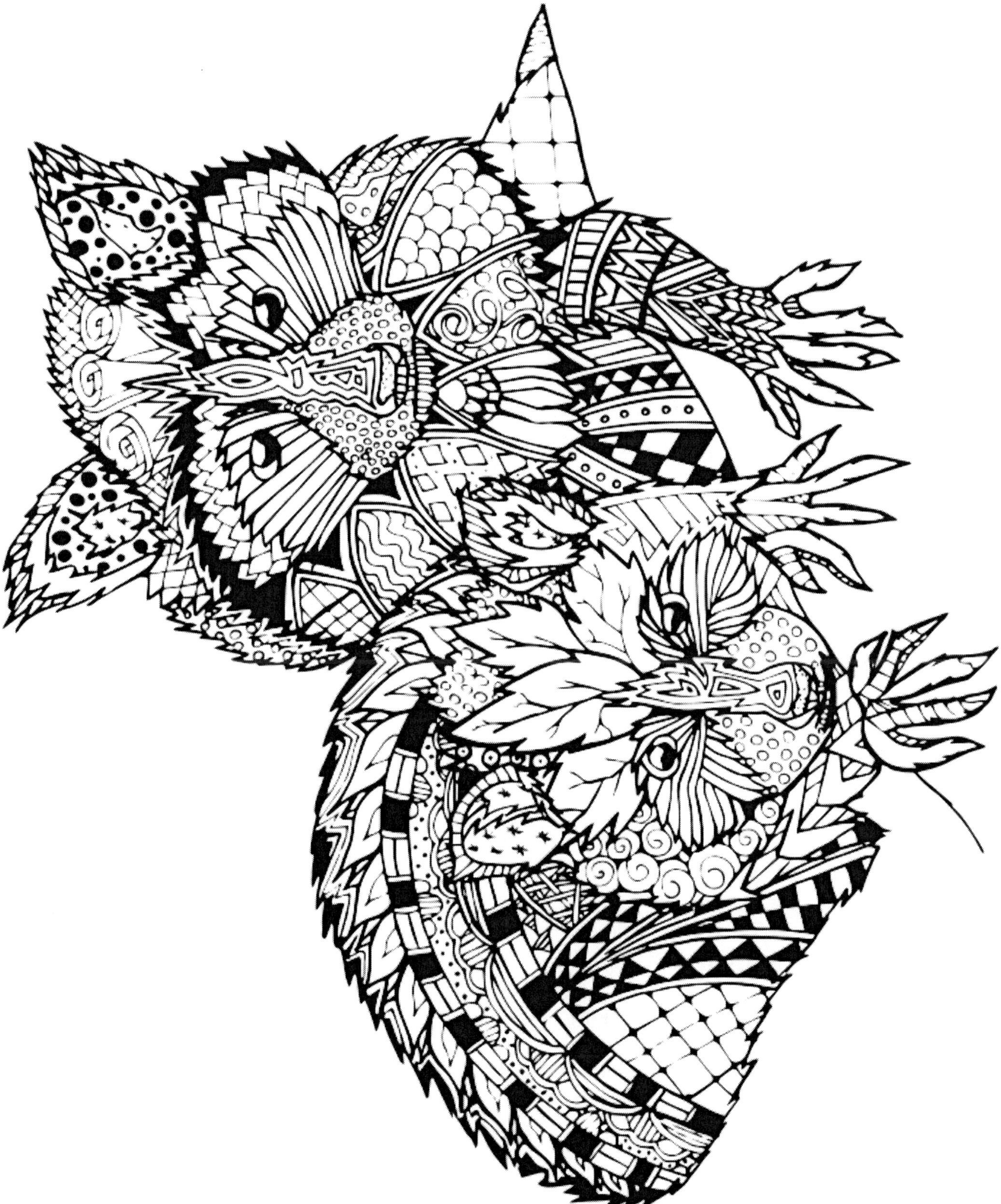

Otter

- **Fun Facts**
  - Male otters are called *boars*, female otters are called *sow,* and baby otters are referred to as *pups*.
  - There are 13 different species of otters, and they all derive from ancestral otters that date back more than 5 million years.
  - Otters are distant cousins to skunks. They are not in anyway related to beavers, although they are often mistaken for them.
  - An otter can hold its breath under water for up to 4 minutes.
  - Otters have been known to hold hands like humans do.
  - Pups and Sows are often close to the same size.
- **What do they Eat?**
  - Otters are mainly carnivorous, surviving mostly on fish.
- **Where They Hang Out**
  - Otters love to swim (like the one illustrated), but they actually spend most of their time on land. Sea Otters are the only species that spend most of their lives in the water. Otters can be found all over the world, with the exception of Australia and Antarctica.
- **Helpful Organization**
  - International Otter Survival Fund

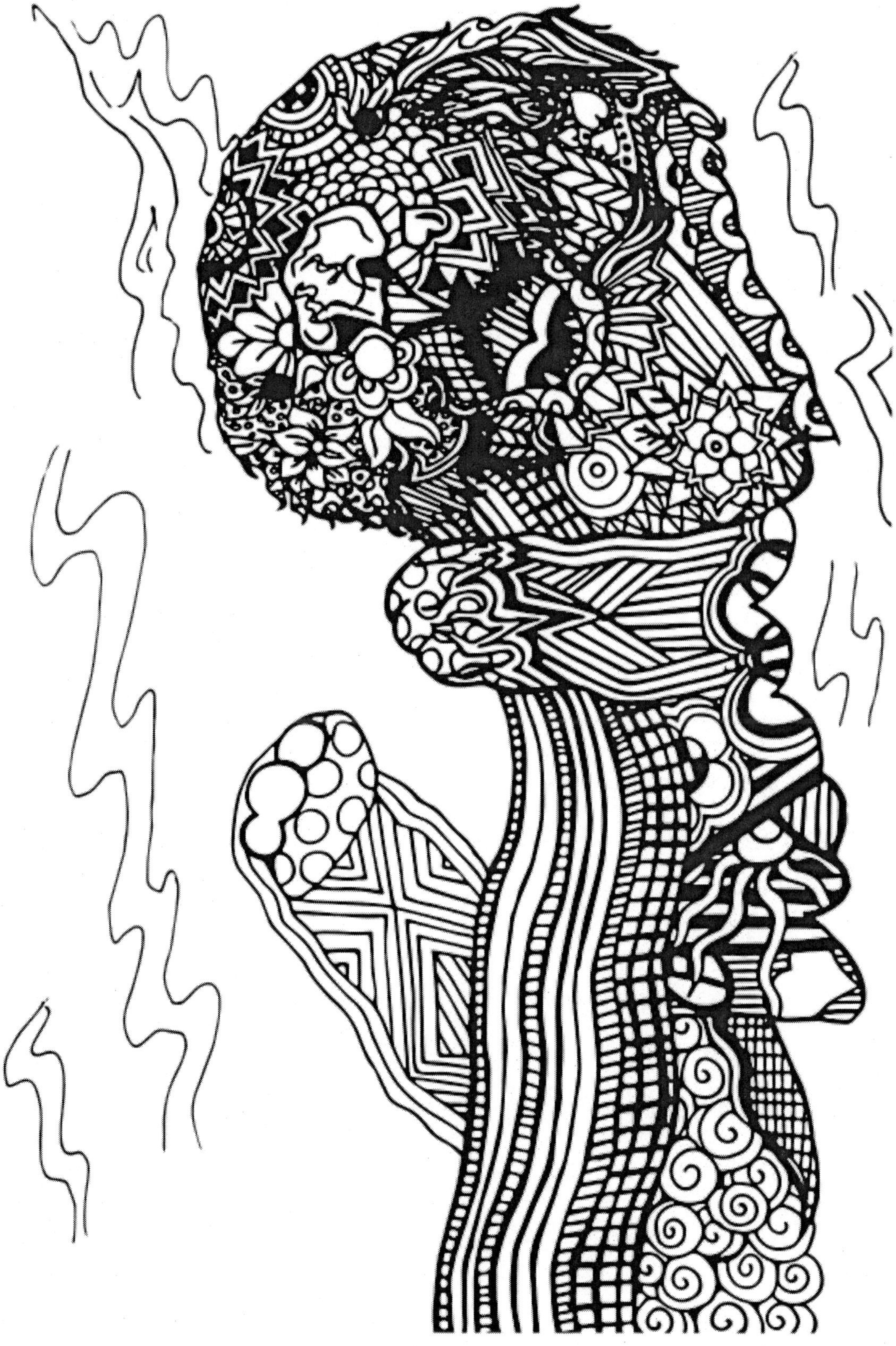

Quokka

- **Fun Facts**
  - Quokkas grow to about 16-21 inches long and are covered with short, coarse, brown and grey fur
  - In 1696, a Dutchman arrived at their island and thought they were large rats. He named the island “Rattennest,” which is Dutch for “Rat's Nest.” The Island is now called Rottnest.
  - Groups of Quokkas live together and are led by dominant males
  - Quokkas are nocturnal creatures.
  - Quokkas are marsupials and give birth to a baby called a joey. They breed twice a year.
  - Quokka joeys live in their mother's pouch for six months.
- **What do they Eat?**
  - Quokkas are herbivores. They eat leaves, grass, stems, and bark. They can survive for long periods of time without food or water. This is because they are able to live off of the fat stored in their tails.
- **Where They Hang Out**
  - They can be found on the island of Rottnest (near Perth, Australia), in Western Australia, and on Bald Island.
  - Quokkas climb trees and like areas with tall grass near water sources
- **Helpful Organization**
  - Quokka Rescue

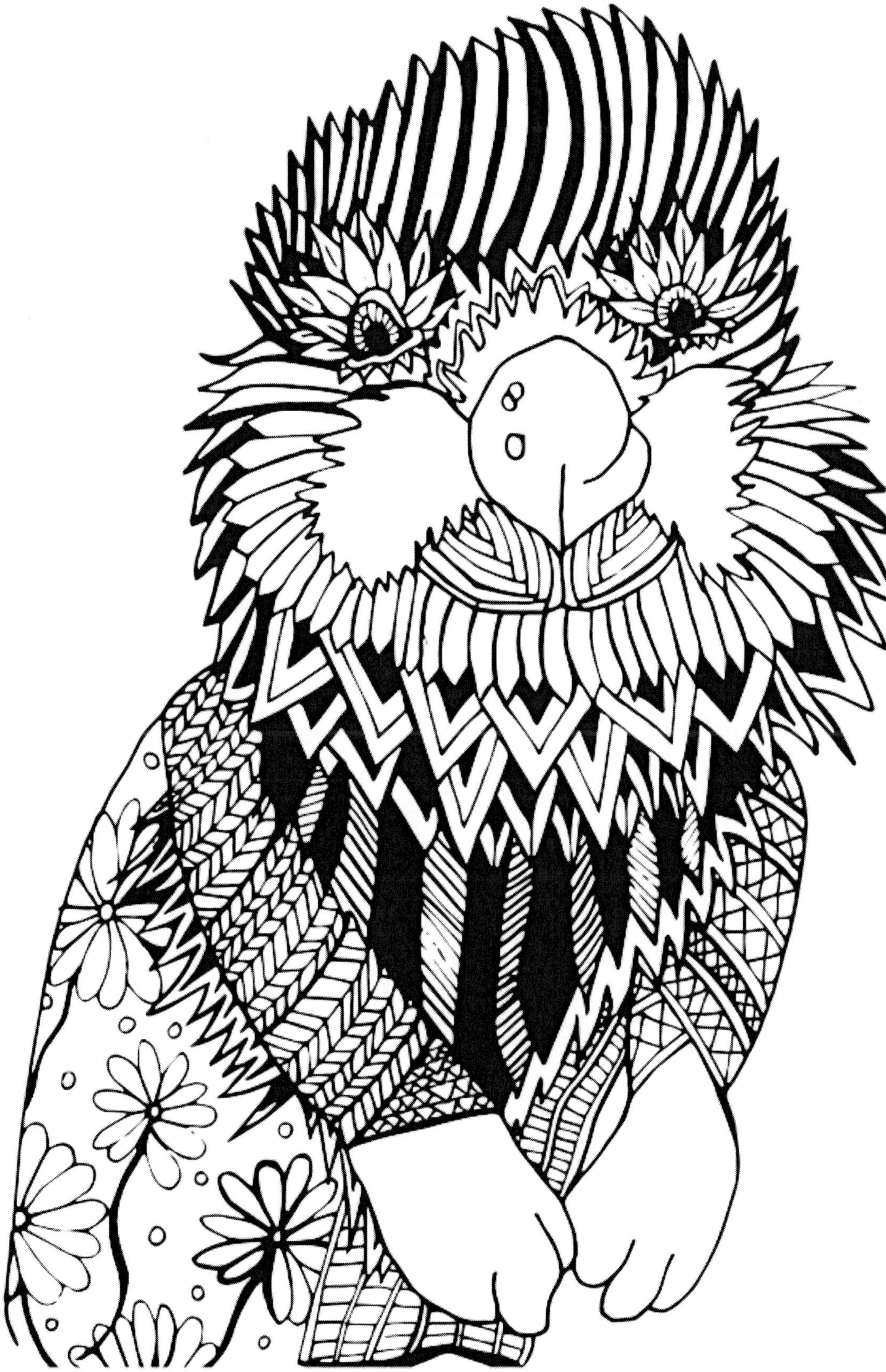

Skunk

- **Fun Facts**
  - A skunk's spray, which it uses as a defensive technique against predators, is nontoxic and can be sprayed out as far as 10 feet.
  - Female skunks give birth between 2 and 10 baby skunks per year.
  - Skunks are mainly nocturnal.
  - Skunks have poor eyesight but they can smell and hear very well.
  - Skunks are usually about the size of a typical house cat.
  - Skunks are really good at digging. They can even burrow underneath buildings by clawing their way through the cracks in foundations.
- **What do they Eat?**
  - Skunks have a diversified diet. They eat fruit, plants, insects, worms, eggs, small mammals, fish, and reptiles. Because they are immune to snake venom, they will also snack on poisonous snakes.
- **Where They Hang Out**
  - Skunks typically live in hollowed out logs, nests built by other animals, and abandoned buildings throughout North, South, and Central America.
- **Helpful Organization**
  - Defenders of Wildlife

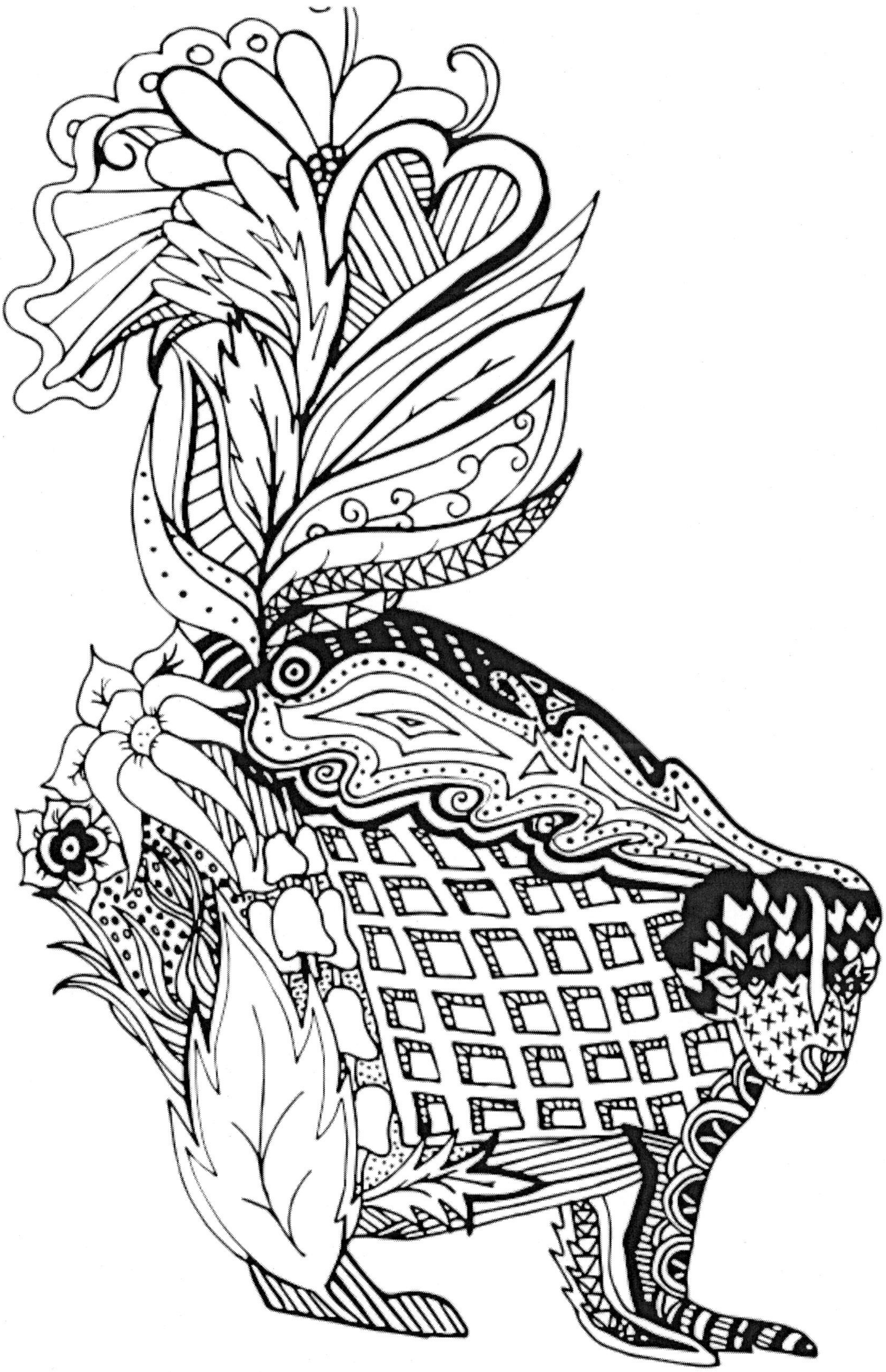

Squirrel

- **Fun Facts**
  - There are over 200 species of squirrels worldwide. The smallest one is only 5 inches long.
  - Baby squirrels are completely blind, so they depend on their mothers for the first several months of their lives.
  - Mother squirrels can have several litters per year.
  - Some squirrels tunnel under the ground and hibernate under the winter.
  - Sometimes ground squirrels work together in groups. When this happens, they warn each other with special calls when danger is approaching.
  - Like many rodents, squirrels have four front teeth that won't stop growing. For that reason, they spend a decent amount of time gnawing on things to file them down.
- **What do they Eat?**
  - Ground squirrels eat nuts, roots, seeds, and leaves. Tree squirrels are partial to acorns, berries, flowers, eggs, baby birds and tree bark. Tree squirrels also snack on tree sap. Flying squirrels eat nuts, fruits, and insects.
- **Where They Hang Out**
  - Squirrels can be found in nearly every country on earth.
- **Helpful Organization**
  - Wildlife Conservation Society

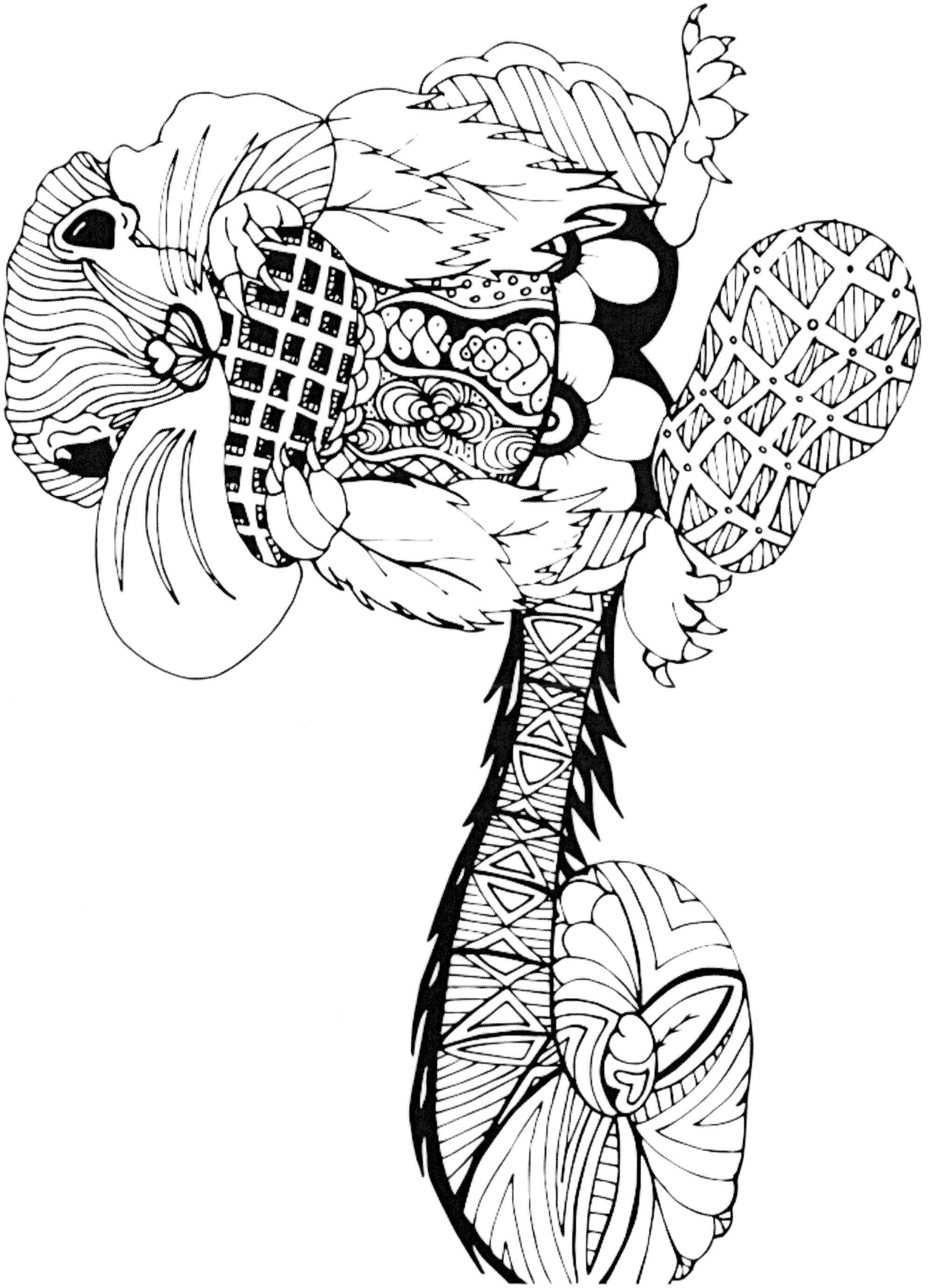

About the Crayon Initiative

- ***What is it?***
  - The Crayon Initiative is a charitable organization that collects unwanted, used and broken crayons and melts them down to create new ones. This keeps the non-biodegradable wax from entering landfills while providing crayons to children who are sick, less fortunate, and in search of creative outlets.
- ***Where do the Crayons Go?***
  - Once they have been recycled and made anew, crayons are sent to schools, hospitals, art programs, and other programs that focus on children.
- ***Where to Send Crayon Donations***
  - Please visit the organization online at www.thecrayoninitiative.org or find them on Facebook and Twitter.
  - You can also contact them at:

The Crayon Initiative

540 Glasgow Circle

Danville, CA. 94526

A Special Thank You

I would like extend a particular thank you to those who have generously donated used and broken crayons to the bulk donation to the Crayon Initiative.

In celebration of this book, the following individuals were generous enough to participate in the first biannual donation on behalf of Artsy Pixie Media, LLC.:

Shannon Vodola

Bianca Deliz

Kirsten Kilgallin

Lajoyce Miller and her students at Elite Prepatory Academy

Cindy Woodward and the folks at The Academy at Julington Creek

About the Artist

- ***Fun Facts About Adamo Publishing & Artsy Pixie Media, Inc***
  - Kara Adamo founded Artsy Pixie Media, LLC in April of 2015. The company is projected to release a stationary line in early 2016.
  - Adamo Publishing is an indie publishing company established in April of 2015.
- ***Where She Hangs Out***
  - Kara Adamo was born in Port Charlotte, FL. She has lived in Denali State Park in Alaska and currently resides in Orlando, Florida. She can be found among her herd, prowling the Thornton Park Wine Walk and Lake Eola.
- ***What Does She Eat?***
  - Kara Adamo has been a pesceterian since 2012. She was a vegetarian between 2009-2012 & was a vegan in 2008. She survives mainly on fish tacos, tuna poke, vegetables, whole grains, and her parents' spaghetti sauce. She also snacks on cupcakes, Kit-Kat bars, and frozen gummy bears. She drinks water, coffee, wine & bourbon.
- ***Other Books***
  - Fancy Grape Juice (published 2015)
- ***Upcoming Projects***
  - Artsy Pixie Stationary
  - Sunlight & Glitter, (A Short Coloring Book)

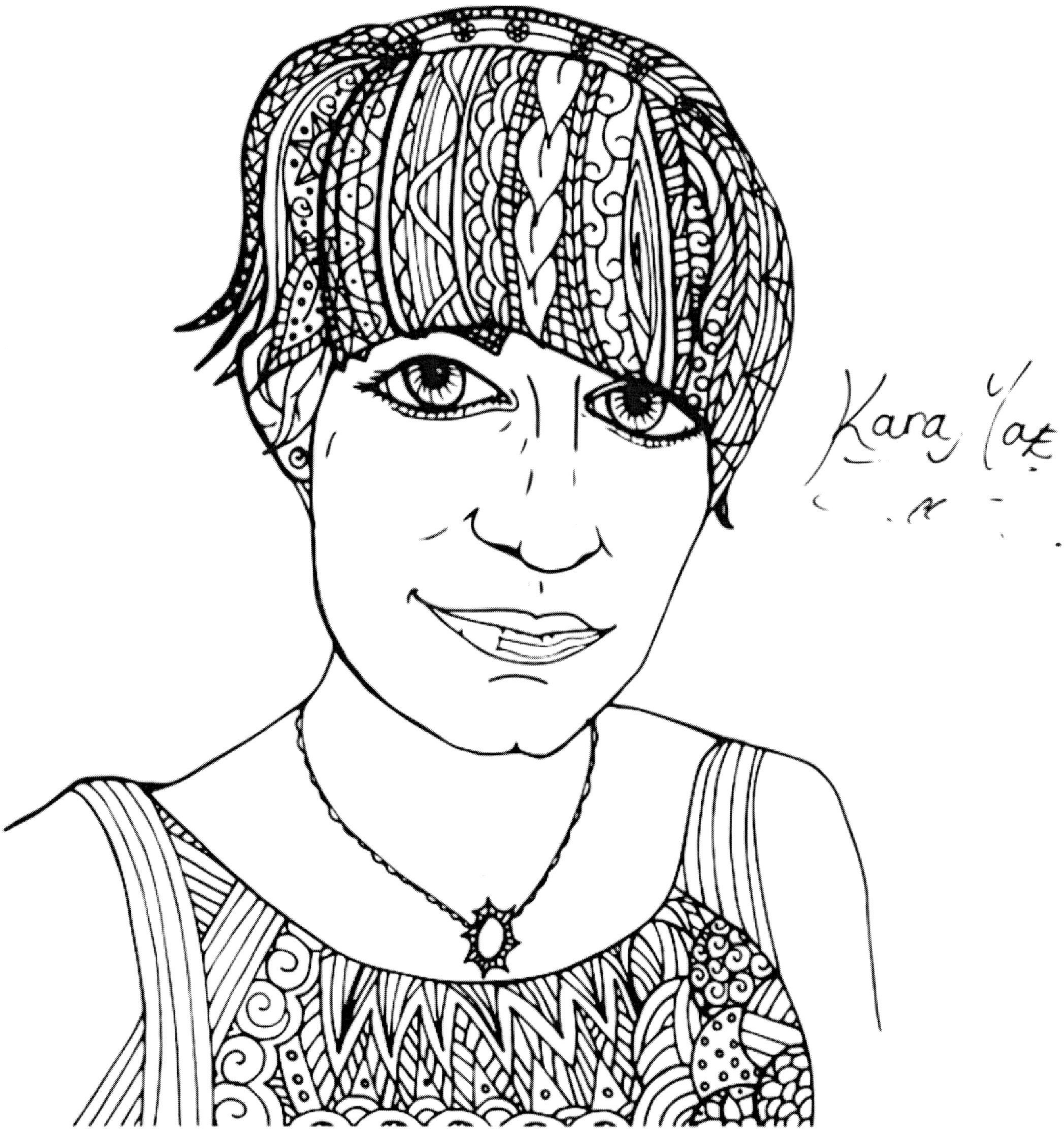
Kara Yat

Media

CPSIA information can be obtained at www.ICGtesting.com
Printed in the USA
BVOW04s1424160116

433167BV00005B/102/P